RIGHT PLACE, RIGHT TIME

RIGHT PLACE, RIGHT TIME

The Ultimate Guide to Choosing a Home
for the Second Half of Life

RYAN FREDERICK

FOREWORD BY PAUL IRVING

JOHNS HOPKINS UNIVERSITY PRESS
Baltimore

© 2021 Johns Hopkins University Press
All rights reserved. Published 2021
Printed in the United States of America on acid-free paper
2 4 6 8 9 7 5 3

Johns Hopkins University Press
2715 North Charles Street
Baltimore, Maryland 21218-4363
www.press.jhu.edu

Library of Congress Cataloging-in-Publication Data

Names: Frederick, Ryan, 1975– author.
Title: Right place, right time : the ultimate guide to choosing a home
    for the second half of life / Ryan Frederick, CEO of SmartLiving 360;
    foreword by Paul Irving, Chairman of the Milken Institute Center for
    the Future of Aging.
Description: Baltimore : Johns Hopkins University Press, 2021. | Includes
    bibliographical references and index.
Identifiers: LCCN 2020057129 | ISBN 9781421442303 (paperback) |
    ISBN 9781421442310 (ebook)
Subjects: LCSH: Older people—Housing—United States. | Aging—
    Social aspects—United States.
Classification: LCC HD7287.92.U54 F74 2021 | DDC
    362.610973—dc23
LC record available at https://lccn.loc.gov/2020057129

A catalog record for this book is available from the British Library.

*Special discounts are available for bulk purchases of this book. For more
information, please contact Special Sales at specialsales@jh.edu.*

*To my wife, Abigail, for her support of my passion
to help people age successfully and for her shared appreciation
for the role of place in helping us thrive*

CONTENTS

FOREWORD

Paul Irving

Ryan Frederick is unusual, in a good way. Unlike so many of his Stanford Business School classmates, Frederick was not excited about a career on Wall Street or awed by the prospect of Silicon Valley stock options. Instead, Frederick was fascinated by homes—particularly homes for our aging population. For many years now, he has studied and talked about the importance of homes and their remarkable impact on the health and well-being of older adults. He knows that place matters—that where one lives often determines how long and how well one lives.

Homes have a special place in our lives. They are our base, the place where we start and end our days. They are familiar and safe, our retreat from the stresses of the outside world. They are a source of pride. But for far too many individuals and families, today's homes simply do not work. Many homes are isolating and unhealthy, lacking the comforts and characteristics that their occupants deserve. Many are inadequate for the realities of a population that is increasingly diverse and rapidly aging.

Frederick has been a passionate advocate for change. With an understanding that demographic challenges and twenty-first-century opportunities call for transformation in design, development, and use, he imagines a different future of living. That is why I was so pleased when Frederick told me that he was writing a book about homes and healthy longevity. He said that he wanted to discuss purposeful living and social connection, that he planned to examine age-restricted and intergenerational models. He had recommendations that deserved to be shared and ideas that called for exploration. It made sense. He was the right correspondent to launch an important conversation at the right time.

Then the COVID-19 pandemic struck.

Across America and the world, people distanced and sheltered in place. Older adults and those with chronic conditions were even more restricted, often dependent on technologies to connect to the outside world. Dwellings became more important than ever, safe harbors in a frightening infectious storm. And in the midst of it all, more and more of us questioned whether our homes were right, whether they suited our needs, whether and how we should change our place.

Frederick's book could not be arriving at a more important time. Many of the topics it covers predate the recent COVID pandemic, but the virus elevates their importance and urgency. For those who are contemplating moves, Frederick raises questions that must be addressed. For those committed to their current place, Frederick probes issues that need to be considered. From tiny houses to advanced technologies to fresh approaches to healthy living, Frederick reveals new thinking about what home means and where home is headed.

In the final analysis, this is a hopeful read, and what is needed to thrive in an era of increasing longevity.

PAUL IRVING is chairman of the Milken Institute Center for the Future of Aging, Distinguished Scholar in Residence at the University of Southern California Leonard Davis School of Gerontology, and chairman of Encore.org.

ACKNOWLEDGMENTS

Writing a book was never on my bucket list. In fact, early in my life, the odds were against it. I excelled at math and science but struggled with reading and writing. Majoring in engineering in college was no accident; I embraced problem sets and labs to avoid reading literature and penning term papers.

But passion won over talent. I was blessed with intergenerational relationships as a youth, and these interactions planted a seed that later took root. I developed a keen interest in how people in the second half of life could thrive and how place helped shape the outcome. I became determined to understand how place can influence well-being, to advise organizations to help them better serve older adults, to create innovative residential models, and, now, to provide information and guidance for individuals to make smart decisions about the role of place in the context of an increasingly long life.

I am grateful for a number of people who helped spark this interest. I was fortunate to know each of my grandparents, spend extended time with them, and even use a winter break during college to stay with my maternal grandparents in their retirement community. My sixth-grade teacher, Marge Zellner, modeled passionate teaching in the classroom and the importance of developing intergenerational relationships in the community. She connected our class with a local retirement community where we played recorders and regularly met an older adult "buddy." Melba Rowlands was my match, a widow in her 80s and kind soul. We continued to get together throughout my middle school years. I treasured this relationship and had no idea of its long-term impact.

A decade or so later, I was blessed to enter the field of housing for older adults. Paul Klaassen, founder and former CEO of Sunrise Senior Living, took a bet on me as an MBA summer intern and granted my wish to live in a retirement community in Atlanta. This experience was invaluable. I am grateful for my friendship with Dan Decker and our work together at CoastWood Senior Housing Partners. Dan challenged the rigor of my thinking, and we bonded over a shared passion for creating better environments to help people thrive. I value his ongoing mentorship. I am grateful for Don Wood, Deirdre Johnson, Greg Timpone, and other talented leaders at Federal Realty Investment Trust for the opportunity to create an innovative place that brings together people of all ages. I am thankful for my various consulting clients across the country and the opportunity to collaborate to make a greater impact on the thousands of people these organizations serve. I am grateful for countless friends, colleagues, and mentors who have directly or indirectly influenced this book, including but not limited to: Bob Kramer, Mike Kerlin, Matt Whitlock, Kurt Read, Mitch Brown, Dr. Bill Thomas, Dean Patricia Davidson, Rick Corcoran Jr., Julie Ferguson, Kathryn Burton Grey, Jacquelyn Kung, Larry Rouvelas, Fred Smith, Anne Tumlinson, Jack Lewin, Jill Vitale-Aussem, David Schless, Bill George, Peter Sims, Mike Metzger, Ken Dychtwald, and many others.

I am also grateful for the encore.org community. Marc Freedman has been mentor and inspiration even before we became friends. His writings on the opportunities of the second half of life, the necessity and joy of intergenerational relationships, and the pitfalls of age segregation abetted by place have deeply influenced my thinking. Being part of his universe has connected me to so many wonderful people. Marci Alboher has encouraged my writing and has been a mentor in content creation and dissemination. Paul Irving has been a valuable source of insight, wisdom, and humor, and I am grateful for his kind foreword to this book. Eunice Lin Nichols has opened up my thinking about the possibilities for intergenerational interactions. I continue to feel supported and inspired by my friends and colleagues in the inaugural Encore Public Voices cohort.

Dr. Henry Cloud, my uber talented and equally hilarious brother-in-law, may be most responsible for this book project. For years, often over a late-night drink, Henry would push me to capture my thoughts in a book to help people directly. It was a war of attrition, but I am thankful that he ultimately won. He opened up his network, including providing an introduction to his book agent, Shannon Marven of Dupree Miller and Associates, who generously helped me craft a book proposal for publishers. Henry has also been instrumental in demystifying the writing process and urging me to put pen to paper. This book would not have happened without his urging, encouragement, and peer pressure.

I am thankful for Johns Hopkins University Press and Barbara Kline Pope for their confidence in this first-time author. Joe Rusko, Heidi Vincent, and Kathryn Marguy were instrumental in giving life to this project and balancing constructive feedback with encouragement. Editing, publishing, and marketing a book during a pandemic is no picnic, and Joe, Heidi, and Kathryn went above and beyond.

I was blown away by insightful comments on the first draft of my book. Molly Singer, former CEO of Capitol Hill Village, is a talented leader, but I had no idea she was also an extraordinary editor. She provided exceptional insights and made the book immeasurably better. Bob Kramer, Mitch Brown, Mike Kerlin, Julie Ferguson, Matt Whitlock, Sara Geber, Jack Lewin, Rick Corcoran Sr., Kate Demase, Pat Demase, Mick Smyer, Kurt Read, Karen Van Dyke, Sally Abrams, Linda Amir, and Fred Smith also provided phenomenal feedback that led to important and substantial changes. I am particularly grateful for Fred Smith's timely emails that helped me see place in an especially broad and meaningful way.

I am grateful for the ongoing encouragement and kind yet critical feedback from my college roommate and best friend, Mike Kerlin. I hope this book motivates him to complete his book projects. Regardless, I can claim to be an author first.

I'd be nowhere without my family. Peter and Gail, my in-laws, have provided constant encouragement. Peter carefully reviewed the manuscript and gave valuable feedback throughout. My parents, Ginny and Ken, dutifully read the manuscript, offered key insights, and were a constant fount of support. In a sense, this work is an outgrowth of my love and care for them. My mom has been particularly good natured as I have told stories about her to audiences nationwide. My hope is that this book can be a valuable resource for my parents and my extended family.

I was warned and subsequently learned that a book project is an endeavor not just for the author but for the whole family. My wife, Abigail, took on more than her fair share of family responsibilities—during a cross-country move and pandemic—to allow me the freedom to complete this project. I will be forever indebted. She also provided key strategic insights on the book. Our kids, Adelaide, Peter, and Andrew, endured far too many dinnertime conversations about the book and the writing process. Needless to say, these teenagers now know a thing or two about healthy aging and the role of place.

I need to direct a special shout-out to my fifteen-year-old daughter. Adelaide expressed so much interest in this project and for writing in general that I hired her as my editor. She did a phenomenal job and helped the book flow logically and become more readable in general. She is a future author. I'm calling it now.

WHY PLACE MATTERS IN THE AGE OF LONGEVITY

Are you prepared to live to 100?

It's not as far-fetched a question as it once was. Centenarians are projected to be one of the fastest-growing demographic groups globally, increasing from less than 100,000 in 1990 to nearly 4 million in 2050.[1] More than half of children born in developed countries today are expected to reach the century mark.[2] Long lives are becoming the norm, especially for those who are educated, take care of themselves, and plan ahead.

The concept of the 100-year life may have already grabbed your attention. Book titles reference it, financial institutions use it in their advertising, and universities have programs to prepare for it. Even my financial advisor assumes a life span of 100 as the default. Yikes!

A long, healthy life should be a good thing. Research bears it out. A happiness curve shows that people around the world are happy as they enter their early 20s, become progressively less so before eventually bottoming out in midlife—late 40s and early 50s—and then reach their highest levels of happiness by their 70s and beyond.[3] There's a reason these later decades are termed the golden years. For many, they are something of tremendous value.

We're all pioneers in the Age of Longevity. There is no foolproof guidebook to help you thrive over the course of a long life—although

I hope this book will become a valuable resource in your journey. We are learning as we go, but it is clear that our best path forward is to understand the key elements that influence longevity and do our best to invest in them.

EARNING ONE'S LONGEVITY

A long life is not a foregone conclusion. The good news is that many of us have the opportunity to earn our longevity. That's right: DNA matters, but other factors far outweigh its significance. By rough numbers, genetics account for at most 30% of our longevity.[4] Ancestral longevity isn't as important a predictor of individual longevity as is commonly believed.[5] In other words, we shouldn't be assured of a long life just because our parents and grandparents have lived long lives. The majority of longevity is a function of individual behaviors coupled with social and environmental factors; things we can control, at least in some measure.

But merely living a long life may not be desirable if those years are spent in poor health or of limited quality. In this sense, health span, or the length of time that one is healthy, is an important consideration. Similarly, wealth span, the length of time that one has financial resources, is a valuable element. Our desired outcome should be a long life span that is matched with an equally long health span and wealth span.

Understandably, significant attention is given to lifestyle choices. Eat healthy foods. Avoid alcohol. Don't smoke. Exercise regularly. Save and invest wisely. Manage costs.

Another important factor that has been overlooked until recently is regular social connection. Increasing social isolation and loneliness have been abetted by our modern culture and made worse during the coronavirus pandemic. Several years ago, a former US surgeon general declared that the United States was facing a loneliness epidemic, the health impact of which could be severe: researchers believe it has the equivalent effect on our health as smoking more than a pack of cigarettes every day.[6] College students and older adults have been found to be the loneliest cohorts.[7]

Purpose matters, too. People with an articulated purpose, particularly in regard to a cause greater than themselves, live longer and healthier lives.[8] Social scientists observe that many people experience a crisis in purpose, often hitting young people and retirees the hardest.

Living longer may be more common in the Age of Longevity, but at the same, it takes effort and dedication to improve the odds of living a long, healthy, and financially secure life.

PLACE MATTERS

The role of place is another factor often overlooked in its impact on our well-being. Country, region, state, metropolitan area, neighborhood, nearby streets, and physical dwelling all play a role in our health. For example, if your state and metropolitan area are economically challenged, your community may not have the financial resources to support successful aging, such as providing key health care and community services. If your neighborhood is unsafe, you are less likely to venture outside of your home and develop connections with neighbors, increasing the risks of social isolation and loneliness. If your physical dwelling provides little natural light, poor air quality, or limited access to nature, your health suffers.

Conversely, the right place can elevate our well-being. It can help promote purpose, facilitate human connection, catalyze physical activity, support financial health, and inspire community engagement. Blue Zones, regions of the world where people live much longer than average, are places that fulfill these requirements.[9] Examples include Sardinia, Italy; Icaria, Greece; Okinawa, Japan; Nicoya Peninsula, Costa Rica; and Loma Linda, California. Each of these places has a high concentration of people who are socially engaged, adhere to healthy diets, prioritize family relationships, and are physically active.

In this sense, our choice of place—where we call home—takes on greater significance than many of us realize. It affects our well-being both directly and an indirectly. If we don't get "home" right, it can be more difficult to make positive life choices. Conversely, if we are in the right home for us, it is easier to live a healthier life. Our choice of home—to the extent that we are able to have a choice—can dramatically shape our life trajectory. It's not an exaggeration to say that place can be a matter of life and death. The COVID-19 pandemic was a tragic reminder of this reality.

At the same time, our definition of home is often too narrow. Home is not just our immediate physical space. Our home is a composite of our country, region, metropolitan area, neighborhood, streets, *and* physical dwelling, such as a house. But home is more than a physical space. It has economic, psychological, and social dimensions.[10]

Home is also a feeling. We are at our best when we have an attachment to home. Living somewhere but never having a sense of home can be reason enough to move. Home should inspire us and be a pathway to become the best possible version of ourselves.

Home has a time dimension, as well. Our connection to home can change without necessarily moving. Friends and neighbors move. Interests shift. Household chores can become too onerous. Physical limitations limit enjoyment or, worse, present risks to our health in an existing home. The perfect home for one point in time can be an awful place later on.

Looked at it in its entirety, home is not just a place to hang our hat. It's not just a financial investment. It's not just where the heart is. Ultimately, home is where the health is.

MY STORY

For the past 15 years, I have focused on the intersection of healthy aging and the role of place. My journey began as a summer intern between years at Stanford's Graduate School of Business working for Sunrise Senior Living, one of the largest senior living companies in the United States. By my request, my internship included living in a retirement community. This experience opened my eyes to the effect of place on older adults. It allowed me to see life through their eyes and better understand their perspectives. It helped me fundamentally appreciate that place matters, in both good and bad ways.

After graduating from business school, my lens broadened as I took on roles as an institutional real estate investment analyst and, later, as an executive for a national senior living operator and developer. Along the way, I analyzed a variety of housing models and their impact on people's lives.

I use these insights in my strategy consulting and real estate development firm, SmartLiving 360. In this capacity, I have advised dozens of organizations from major real estate development firms and multi-billion-dollar investment firms to leading health systems and senior living providers on matters of strategy and product innovation. I co-developed an intergenerational apartment project in a mixed-use walkable suburban area of Washington, DC. The projected has garnered national attention as an innovative approach to developing and operating an age-friendly apartment community. I have shared my ideas for the future of housing through various national keynote presentations, blogs, and podcasts.

Along this journey, I developed a reputation as a go-to resource for questions related to place and healthy aging among friends and family. I gained an appreciation for the complexities of each person's situation and how challenging finding the right place can be for older adults and their families. Many people lack knowledge on options and often don't know where to begin. I also learned that many people question the limited housing options available. In response, I launched a monthly consumer blog to help disseminate helpful information.

In recent years, there has been an increasing societal appreciation for the significance of place throughout life. Raj Chetty, an economics professor at Harvard University and director of Opportunity Insights, has harnessed big data to demonstrate how life expectancy can differ by decades based on zip code.[11] In addition, AARP launched the AARP Livability Index for public policy professionals and planners to make better-informed policy decisions about place to improve livability across the age spectrum. Even health care policy professionals began to speak more about the effect of social determinants of health, highlighting the role of place and living environment.

Then COVID-19 hit. The pandemic crystallized for many the critical role of place in health. In some cases, place worked well—one could be physically distant yet still connected to others and able to receive needed goods and services. In other cases, place either introduced higher risks of infection or further aggravated pangs of social isolation and loneliness. The pandemic served as a wake-up call that where you live matters a lot.

I was prompted to ask: What if more people better understood the role of place as they aged, and in turn were able to make better-informed decisions? This book is an effort to answer that question by turning my passion and insider knowledge about the role of place and healthy aging into something instructive and insightful for individuals and their families.

PURPOSE OF THIS BOOK

This book is written for people who are interested in making decisions to optimize the odds of living a long, healthy, and financially secure life. If you care enough to watch your diet, exercise regularly, and save responsibly, then you ought to carefully consider your home at every stage of life.

One of the realities of a 100-year life is that there are lots of stages—some predictable and some less so. Of course, the early years are more predictable. Baby, toddler, preschool, elementary school, middle school, high school, and launched into the world. From there, the divergence starts from levels of higher education to jobs and careers to relationships and families to health and so on.

Unlike when we are younger and go through life stages as cohorts of peers, life transitions as we get older are often managed alone or with a partner and family, if we are fortunate. And there is no guidebook.

Each transition presents a decision about place. Making a decision about the best place to live for a given moment in time becomes not an occasional undertaking but one that presents itself often enough to become a core competency. In other words, you'd better be good at it. The average person moves about 12 times throughout the course of their life.[12]

While home affects health at any stage of life, this book is designed for people navigating the second half of life. It is for empty nesters who are evaluating place without kids in the picture. It is for retirees looking to write a new chapter where a change of location may be part of the story. It is for older people who are concerned about being in the best place as health concerns become more prominent. It is for singles and solo agers, those without adult children and family, where planning for longevity becomes even more essential.[13] It is for couples to map out a path together. It is for advance planners—those as young as in their 30s—who wish to commit to a place for the long haul. The book is also intended to be a key resource for adult children who are looking for ways to best support their parents and loved ones. A reader may benefit both directly and indirectly from its content and calls to action.

In this book, we read stories about people who have made big decisions about their choice of place. Some of these decisions were the right ones at the right time. Others were not. Some places changed from being a good fit to later becoming detrimental to one's well-being. Indeed, most often, it is the decision *not* made that ends up being the most costly. This book underscores the importance of developing the discipline of consciously choosing the right place and doing so with a broad view of home and its impact on overall well-being.

HOW TO USE THIS BOOK

This book is organized to help you understand the significance of place, evaluate the fit of your current home, explore a growing list of options, and take action. Part I helps you evaluate whether you are in the right place for now. It provides context for the role of place in the broader setting of longevity and well-being, and it offers a self-evaluation tool to gauge the appropriateness of your current home. The section ends with a rebuke of the term "aging in place" and points out its inadequacy as an optimal strategy for most people.

Parts II and III unpack specific options for place. They start with considerations for regions, metropolitan areas, and neighborhoods and move to specific housing models ranging from conventional single-family homes and apartments to age-restricted housing and senior living to emerging models and considerations of living with or near family.

Part IV focuses on how housing is changing, particularly from technology, health, and health care perspectives. Significant advances are expected in these areas in the years ahead, and planners should factor these shifts into their thinking before making irreversible decisions.

Part V prompts the reader to take specific action by either making the most of their current living situation or launching a process to select, move to, and settle into a new place. The book closes by challenging readers to choose the right place at the right time.

The book is designed to be read sequentially, but more than that, it is a resource to serve your needs. Part I is to be read first and in its entirety, as it creates the foundation for the book. Readers may wish to skip to specific sections of interest in parts II, III, and IV. Part V, coupled with the self-evaluation from earlier in the book, is critical to take specific action.

This book is intended to be an ongoing resource as life circumstances change. A reader may use it to help with not only a particular transition today but also any future transitions. In fact, part of my philosophy is that each of us needs to develop a habit of regularly evaluating the appropriateness of our current place and exercising the discipline to choose the right place at the right time.

FOLLOWING MY OWN ADVICE

We recently relocated our family, including a teenager and two pre-teens, from the Mid-Atlantic to Texas. It was a tough decision. We loved our old neighborhood and house. We had developed rich friendships, and it was a place where our kids had thrived. The Mid-Atlantic was a place where my wife had started a small business and I was able to expand my business.

But as we evaluated our situation, we were convinced that moving was the right decision. We wished to be closer to family on the West Coast and wanted better schools for our children. My wife wanted to sell her business and switch careers, and I was looking for a place where I could continue to create age-friendly communities while more easily traveling throughout the country. At the same time, we were becoming increasingly concerned about the trajectory of our existing place.

Identifying where to move was more challenging. We researched online, spoke with friends, and read articles about various states and metropolitan areas. We took reconnaissance trips to better understand places firsthand. We settled upon Austin for a host of reasons, including its central proximity in the country, family-friendly environment, and entrepreneurial vibe, among other factors. We chose our neighborhood and house based on the quality of the schools and sense of connection among residents. We were intentional about finding a place that would positively influence our collective well-being.

While our kids featured prominently in our decision, we had an eye toward a place that could serve as home once we became empty nesters. Our vision was to settle somewhere that would have the potential for us to live and thrive for decades to come, even if our particular housing choices changed over time. At this point, we're not sure if our life in Austin will turn out as we envision, but we're hopeful that it may. In a number of respects, our process incorporated elements that empty nesters and older adults would consider when evaluating a change of place.

The change wasn't easy. It was emotional to leave our home, as we were overwhelmed by gratitude and loss. Moving to a new place with few existing friends was an exciting adventure on good days and exhausting and lonely on bad ones. COVID-19 made settling into our new community challenging. We reminded ourselves that just because it was hard didn't mean it wasn't the right decision.

A SEND-OFF

Planning is particularly important in the Age of Longevity. But so is courage. Knowing what you should do and actually doing it can be two entirely different things. This tension can be particularly acute as we get older and changes are harder to make.

Regardless of stage of life, though, home is important. As we aim to live long, healthy and prosperous lives, we should look to maximize all components of our well-being, including the role of place. As you read this book, think about how each factor ties into your life and the lives of loved ones. Understanding is the first step toward changing your life for the better.

PART I

ARE YOU IN THE RIGHT PLACE FOR NOW?

Part I helps you evaluate whether you are in the right place for the time being. It provides context for the role of place in the broader setting of longevity and well-being and provides a self-evaluation tool to gauge the appropriateness of your current home. The section ends with a rebuke of the term "aging in place" and points out its inadequacy as an optimal strategy for most people.

CHAPTER 1

PLACE AS A KEY COMPONENT OF SUCCESSFUL AGING

I enjoy cooking. One of the things that I've learned over the years is that the best dishes result from a good recipe paired with good ingredients. A tasty recipe with poor ingredients won't get you very far; likewise, it's a challenge for quality ingredients to overcome a bad recipe.

This dynamic is reflected in the context of healthy aging. As the science of aging progresses, we are learning more about the recipe for healthy aging. The ingredients of healthy aging are based more in lifestyle choices and environment than DNA. If we follow the right steps and make the right choices, we have a much higher chance of achieving a promising result.

The Gallup Organization, an analytics and advisory company, conducted a comprehensive study of people across more than 150 countries and found five universal, interconnected elements that shape our well-being: purpose, social connection, physical well-being, financial well-being, and community well-being.[1] The importance of place is embedded in the attribute of community well-being.[2] Gallup went a step further and partnered with Healthways, a population health company, to create the Gallup-Healthways Well-Being Index. This annual survey evaluates people's well-being on the basis of the five key elements across all states and major metropolitan areas of the

United States. It's an acknowledgment that place matters significantly in healthy aging.

PURPOSE

My late friend Charlotte Siegel excelled at purpose. Charlotte lived a 100-year-long life, and her commitment to purpose no doubt had a significant role in her longevity. Charlotte was born at a time when few women went to college and far fewer obtained graduate degrees. She followed her call to social work, psychiatric work in particular, and worked diligently, completing her graduate degree while raising two young children with her husband, who worked full-time. Charlotte found purpose in raising her family as well as in using her talents to better the lives of a much broader community, something virtually unheard of in the 1940s.

Her passion fueled her for decades. She eschewed traditional retirement and made contributions to the field for more than 70 years. She saw clients into her 90s. Patients came to her retirement community for her services.

Collaborating with colleagues was one of her career joys. In her mid-90s, Charlotte was the recipient of an honorary award for her contributions to the field of clinical social work from the California Society of Clinical Social Work. She was an inspiration, but she was also an active member. She was instrumental in bringing high-profile speakers to the organization, including Stanford University professor of psychology Carol Dweck. Dr. Dweck is nationally acclaimed for her contributions to a theory of intelligence characterized as the growth mindset, one that claims people's talents and abilities can be developed through effort and persistence.[3] Charlotte is a 100-year life case study of the growth mindset.

Part of Charlotte's success was living an integrated life. In Charlotte's words, "My social work self, my clinical self, my total being self, they are all wrapped together. There isn't a separate clinician and separate Charlotte Siegel. It's all a part of the definition and a part of what I am able to give to clients who come to see me—a sense of life moving for me and for them."[4] Longevity was probably not foremost on her mind when she pursued her calling in her 20s, but it's not happenchance that she lived such a long and vital life. Her purpose of serving others and contributing to her field gave her meaning daily.

We know that purpose is important at any age. Purpose is one of the best predictors of happiness.[5] In this context, purpose is defined as the sources of meaning that are both goal oriented and motivated by a desire to make a difference in the world beyond one's self. People who have a defined purpose tend to be both psychologically and physically healthier than those who do not.[6] Individuals without purpose are more likely to suffer from depression, boredom, loneliness, and anxiety.[7]

Purpose not only helps people avoid negative states, it also promotes positive states, such as optimism, hope, and life satisfaction, and it has been shown to have tremendous impacts on health.[8] Those with purpose tend to have lower cholesterol as well as lower rates of obesity, mild cognitive impairment, and Alzheimer's disease.[9]

One of the challenges is that living with purpose can get harder with age. For many of life's earlier stages, purpose is more clearly defined and socially acceptable. Find a fulfilling career. Provide financial security for family. Be a supportive partner. But as we approach midlife and beyond, purpose can be elusive, particularly if some of the earlier goals were met. Retirement can add fuel to the fire. The word "retire" means to withdraw. A move to retirement can be a move away from purpose, particularly the type of purpose that is goal oriented and motivated to make a difference beyond one's self.

In the age of longevity, a challenge and opportunity is to make sure purpose is present at every stage of life. Charlotte's story is inspirational but unique. Few of us are likely to have a calling that provides meaning for many decades. It's more likely that sources of purpose will need to change and evolve. It may involve finding a new passion. Perhaps it is pursuing an encore career. An encore career is work in the second half of life that combines continued income, greater personal meaning, and social impact.[10] I have one friend nearing retirement age who is focusing his energies on combating climate change and has created tools to help people make a difference. Paid opportunities in an encore career can be found in a variety of fields such as education, government, and various nonprofits.

Opportunities for greater purpose past midlife may also be found through relationships. It may involve caregiving for a loved one or looking after grandchildren. I know of people who have intentionally carved out time for extended family on a regular basis and have created enough flex in their schedule to be available in a greater way should needs arise. There are also ample opportunities to come alongside neighbors to develop deeper and more meaningful relationships that can provide additional purpose for all involved.

What's clear is that purpose is essential for longevity and, according to the research, that this purpose is pursued and found daily.

SOCIAL CONNECTION

My friend Ken should be dead. Over the years, a group of us would run the infamous Bay to Breakers race in San Francisco. It has been named the largest footrace by the Guinness Book of World Records, but it is as much a party as a run, with many participants donning costumes or nothing at all. Nevertheless, for those who do run, particularly if it falls on a warm spring day, the 10-mile course can be a challenge. Such was the case for Ken, a fit runner in his early 50s.

In 2010, Ken was running the race alone. Immediately upon crossing the finish line, Ken collapsed. Fortunately, a good Samaritan noticed him on the ground. Ruth, a doctor, jumped in and provided CPR. Once resuscitated, he was rushed to the hospital. Ken had suffered a sudden cardiac arrest. Ruth had saved his life.

His friends mobilized. A friend sent a group email to Ken's friends asking for help. One group of friends tracked down his car, and another cared for his beloved golden retriever, Riley. Other friends headed to the hospital and were on hand when it was decided that Ken needed an emergency quadruple bypass surgery. A couple reached out to Ken's parents and met them along the freeway before escorting them to the hospital. Visitors bearing gifts and food streamed into the hospital and later his home. Several friends even manned his painting business for a number of months during his unexpected absence. It takes a village.

While Ken was blessed to have a medical professional on the spot at the time of his cardiac arrest, it was his network of friends that he built over time who supported him at a moment's notice and aided his recovery. His network of diverse, committed friends is no accident. Over the years, Ken, who has never married, built a cadre of close friends, some his peers, others older, and plenty younger. Even as a shy extrovert, he has made a conscious decision to reach out to people on a consistent and deliberate basis. We recently celebrated the tenth anniversary of Ken's near-death experience. Close to 100 people participated, including friends that Ken made since his health scare.

Ken intentionally builds friendships and stays connected. He works at it. He never forgets your birthday and he calls, not texts. He knows the important things about you, and he'll be sure to ask about them. He's generous with his time and resources. More often than not, he opens his house to visitors, whether a friend or even a stranger. I can tell you, he's hard to shake. And his friends like it this way. By showing this level of interest in and care for others, he has benefited from reciprocal relationships. For a single male in midlife, Ken has a network of strong relationships that would make people of any age and stage envious.

It comes as no surprise that Ken later befriended his heroine, Ruth. They light up when they see each other. And his heart attack alerted him to the importance of CPR training; he's since become a national spokesperson for the American Heart Association.

Ken's story is a helpful illustration for all of us. Our health and well-being depend heavily on our network of social connections.

Dr. Vivek H. Murthy, the former US surgeon general and author of *Together: The Healing Power of Human Connection in a Sometimes Lonely World*, agrees. He has been outspoken about the importance of social connection and has called out loneliness as a national health epidemic. In his time as a physician, he found that "the most common pathology [he] saw was not heart disease or diabetes; it was loneliness."[11]

Loneliness has been found to be as harmful as smoking 15 cigarettes a day and can increase the risk of premature death by as much as 30%.[12] Loneliness is subjective. It is the distressing feeling that accompanies discrepancies between one's desired and actual social relationships.[13] People who are physically isolated tend to be lonely, though not necessarily. Some people can be around others and still feel lonely.[14]

Social isolation is similar to but different than loneliness. Social isolation is an objective measure of the number of contacts and interactions one has.[15] It is about the quantity and not the quality of relationships. Some may prefer less social interaction. Like loneliness, however, low levels of social isolation have a negative impact on health.

Pandemics, such as the COVID-19 outbreak, pose a particular threat. They create a lose-lose scenario for older adults. On one hand, socializing with others in person is valuable but presents health threats. On the other hand, self-quarantining may protect health but increases physical isolation, which heightens the risks of social isolation and loneliness. Video calls may help, but in-person, face-to-face contact is shown to have a far greater beneficial effect on our health.[16]

Technology is a mixed bag when it comes to social connection. Email, video calls, texting, and social media allow us to connect with people near and far. But some of these tools, social media in particular, have been found to reduce a sense of well-being when used in high doses. Its usage offers the perception of meaningful social interaction, but the nature of the connection is no substitute for real-world interaction.[17] Maintaining a balance of online and in-person contacts seems to be the healthiest approach.

It can be difficult in midlife and beyond to have strong social connections. Circumstances can change, such as leaving social circles associated with a job, physically moving into a new living environment, or losing friends and family, including a partner. Beyond that, life can get busy, and time with friends can get crowded out. No matter the circumstances, however, intentionality to maintain and create friendships is critical to thriving in a 100-year life.

PHYSICAL WELL-BEING

Sufferfest is a biannual gathering that brings together middle-aged men from across the United States for a day of nearly unimaginable pain (suffer) and outdoor adventure and camaraderie (fest[ival]).[18] Sufferfest adventures have covered the country from the Pacific Crest Trail in California to the Grand Canyon to the Appalachian Trail in the Mid-Atlantic and more. I joined for a trip to Bryce National Park in Utah, covering 45 miles and 10,000 vertical feet. These adventures are not easy.

Sufferfest is the creation of two close friends, Rick and Ben. In the late 1990s, they competed together in the Eco Challenge in Argentina, an adventure race that spanned multiple days straight of racing involving trekking, kayaking, mountaineering, and more. One might think that now that they were in their mid-40s, they would have moved on from this chapter in their lives. They did not, and instead decided to make ridiculous adventures at least slightly more accessible to others.

Neither Rick nor Ben is a researcher in longevity, but both men embody the current literature on physical well-being. They emphasize the importance of physically demanding effort with others. They even have a mission statement: "Sufferfest is for men to spend time together in the outdoors doing transformatively hard adventures which forge deep relationships." It is a good example of how multiple ingredients for healthy aging—in this case physical well-being and social connection—can be tackled in tandem.

If physical exercise, particularly demanding physical exercise that promotes fitness, was a drug, it would be a blockbuster. Exercise has been shown to have an impact on our physical well-being in a plethora of ways, from strengthening muscles to improving heart conditions to sharpening minds.[19, 20] These benefits have been shown to have an impact on all age groups. In fact, some of the biggest benefits of exercise accrue to those in middle age and beyond. There's also research that suggests that there are significant benefits if one moves from a sedentary to an active lifestyle later in life. In other words, you don't have to be a lifelong Sufferfester like Rick or Ben to enjoy the benefits of exercise.

Not all exercise is the same, however. While studies indicate there are benefits from a regular brisk 10-minute walk, the biggest gains are from truly pushing yourself: interval workouts, hills, and the like. More intense workouts that materially improve conditioning have been shown to improve cellular health, rebuild muscle, and elevate strength. Such training also appears to improve memory and ward off cognitive decline.[21,22] There is also a strong case for resistance training, either with bands or weights, to build muscle and improve bone density. Studies also suggest that it can have a positive impact on memory.[23]

Team sports are linked to increased longevity, too. A Copenhagen City Heart Study found that the best types of exercise for improving life expectancy are athletic activities that involve others.[24] Tennis, badminton, and soccer outperformed often solitary strenuous pursuits like running, swimming, and cycling. In fact, regular tennis players were shown to live about 10 years longer than those with more sedentary lifestyles and more than 5 years longer than joggers. Sufferfesters benefit from the comradery of the one-day event, but more significantly, most participants train for months with others in their area, often for hours at a time.

A healthy diet could be a blockbuster drug in its own right. A poor diet, particularly one lacking plant-based foods and containing too much salt, is now the leading root cause of death globally—exceeding smoking, high blood sugar, or any other single factor.[25] Unhealthy diets drive heart disease, type 2 diabetes, and many forms of cancer. Moreover, a poor diet increases inflammation, which, if experienced on a chronic basis, is linked to heart disease, diabetes, cancer, depression, and dementia.[26] Inflammation increases with age—sometimes referred to as "inflammaging"—making it even more important to manage our diet as we get older.

We are learning more about the role of a healthy diet to help prevent dementia. The Mediterranean-DASH Intervention for Neurodegenerative Delay (MIND) diet, which is a variant of the Mediterranean Diet, focuses on eating whole grains, berries, vegetables—especially green, leafy ones—olive oil, poultry, and fish. Researchers have found that strict adherence to the MIND diet for older adults resulted in a decreased risk of Alzheimer disease, and even mild adherence to the diet has shown to have positive effects.[27]

Sleep is an often overlooked component of physical well-being. Dr. Matthew Walker, director of the Sleep and Neuroimaging Lab at the University of California, Berkeley, claims, based on dozens of research studies, that sleep is the single most effective thing we can do to reset our brain and body health each day.[28] Sleep helps cement positive memories, mollify painful ones, and meld past and present knowledge, inspiring creativity. Conversely, insufficient sleep can wreak havoc on health. Insufficient sleep, or routinely sleeping less than six or seven hours a night, demolishes the immune system, more than doubling the risk of cancer, and increases the odds of diabetes, heart disease, and dementia, among other effects. Too little sleep also makes it more difficult to manage stress and anxiety. It's no exaggeration to say that not getting enough sleep can kill you.

A full night's sleep is important at any age, but it gets harder to achieve as we get older. In midlife and beyond, we witness a reduction in sleep quantity, quality, and efficiency. By age 70, an individual has lost about 80% to 90% of the deep sleep enjoyed as a teenager. Further, sleep efficiency—the amount of actual sleep time versus bedtime—falls from 95% to 70%–80%. Therefore, to achieve 8 hours of sleep, we need 10 or more hours of bedtime. In addition, there is a change in circadian rhythm; older adults tend to tire earlier, leading to earlier bedtimes. Hence the "early bird" dinner special at your local restaurant.

Managing these changes as we age is critical. Lower sleep efficiency triggers higher mortality risk, worse physical health, greater likelihood of depression, reduced energy, and lower cognitive function, typified by forgetfulness. In some cases, forgetfulness may be more linked to poor sleep than a mental condition.

Taken in its entirety, being physically active, maintaining a healthy diet, and sleeping well are all important contributors to physical and cognitive well-being. It's even better when combined with social engagement, as Sufferfesters can validate.

FINANCIAL WELL-BEING

My grandfather, part of the Greatest Generation, was a planner. As a teenager, he experienced—or, more accurately, survived—the Great Depression, when for a time he was the primary breadwinner for his family delivering newspapers. He later became the owner of a small business. Although he officially retired in his 60s like many of his peers, he was always financially planning. His experience of scarcity and uncertainty associated with the Great Depression never left him. He managed his assets carefully, made sure to maximize his pension benefits, and read the *Wall Street Journal* daily to have an eye on the present and future. He taught me about investing when I was in elementary school; I won a mock stock-trading competition thanks to his coaching. In the end, his successful planning enabled my grandparents to pursue interests and cover health care costs once their health faded. They enjoyed the benefits of financial well-being and a wealth span that was as long as their life span.

Sometimes I wonder how my grandfather would plan in today's environment. How does anyone financially plan to live to 100?

Likely none of us really knows the answer, but it is common knowledge that good financial planning matters. Financial resources enable investments in health, such as traveling with friends, eating healthy foods, and living in a safe place. Wealth also creates a buffer for unexpected costs in life, such as those related to failing health.

Financial resources increase wealth span but also positively influence life span and health span.[29] Wealthy women live, on average, 33 disability-free years after age 50; for men, that figure is 2 years less.

In both cases, this is about a decade longer of disability-free living as compared to those who are poor.

Today, more of the financial planning for a longer life is falling on individuals. Most employers have discontinued guaranteed benefit pensions in favor of 401(k) and other forms of defined contribution accounts. This shifts responsibility for investment returns from the employer to individuals. Further, government pensions are under pressure, with some likely to be restructured, and social security is projected to be insolvent by 2035.[30] It is unlikely that the social security entitlement will disappear, but the qualifying age for benefits may rise.

One of the challenges with retirement planning is that even though we often know what to do, we have a hard time doing it. Take saving, for example. Studies indicate that people know they should start early and save about 25% of their income annually. But in practice, they often don't start saving until later in life, losing out on the full impact of compounding investment returns. In aggregate, people only save about 5% of their income each year. Merrill Lynch calls this the Intention-Action Gap.[31] There are a number of reasons for this dynamic, but part of the challenge is that psychologically, we have a hard time relating to our future selves. In fact, studies indicate that we can relate to our future selves about as much as we can relate to a stranger.[32]

Life circumstances can make it more challenging, too. Today, singleness is more common. Divorce among those aged 55 and over, called "gray divorce," is increasing and often has significant financial implications.[33] After a divorce, household income typically drops by 25% for men and more than 40% for women.[34] These circumstances can push pre-retirees and retirees closer to needing financial support, including from family. Solo agers, those aging without kids, must be particularly careful because they don't have family to fall back on.

What many of us desire is financial security that offers peace of mind. Financial security has three times the impact of your income alone on overall well-being.[35] Financial security is a function of net worth, annual income, and annual expenditures. Net worth is straight-forward to calculate: add the value of various assets, such as cash, stocks, and real estate holdings, and subtract liabilities, such as loans. There is additional complexity and uncertainty in projecting annual income and annual expenditures.

One approach to improve financial security is to work longer. Near-ly half of those 65 and older currently work, have worked, or expect to pursue work into retirement age.[36] But this option may not be a given.[37] Age discrimination in the workplace, or ageism, is prevalent. About three out of five older workers have seen or experienced ageism in the workplace, and 76% of these older works see age discrimination as a hurdle to finding a new job.[38] Plus, training or additional skills may be required to compete for jobs in the economy of the future. The expectation to work longer may not be realistic.

There is also uncertainty in annual costs. Some of the uncertainty rests outside of ourselves. We may have friends and family, such as a parent or child, who require financial support. But the primary risk is our health. Poor health can increase costs as well as affect the abil-ity to work and enjoy life. Note that 33% of 65-year-olds may never need long-term care support, but 20% will need it for longer than five years.[39] Long-term care is expensive and not reimbursed by Medicare. Perhaps it is not surprising that while financial security is the leading worry for decades, health concerns become the leading worry at age 70 and beyond.[40]

The complexity of financial planning for a 100-year life makes seek-ing professional financial advice particularly important. More sophis-ticated online financial tools and services are evolving, too. One thing is clear: assuming that the government will be able to provide for a comfortable, long life is not a viable strategy.

PLACE

Place has a significant impact on our health and well-being. In its broad definition, place encompasses region, state, metropolitan area, neigh-borhood, and physical dwelling. Place has both direct and indirect impacts on a person's life. The best place elevates the other elements of well-being described above—purpose, social connection, physical well-being, and financial well-being—and positively influences well-being in and of itself.

I have been fortunate to experience the benefits of place firsthand. During the years of raising three kids under 5 years old, my wife and I lived in the Presidio, a former US Army military fort located in the northern part of San Francisco. In the mid-1990s, the fort was transferred to the National Park Service, and a public-private partnership was formed to manage the property. Our young family was part of an initial cohort of renters in homes that previously served as officer quarters.

We loved living in an urban park. We walked to playgrounds, schools, restaurants, and trails. I bicycled to work downtown, largely using dedicated bike lanes. Our duplex was one of a half dozen on a cul-de-sac at the top of a hill with a view of the Golden Gate Bridge. Yards were small, but we shared a patch of green in the middle of the circle. This patch became the de facto meeting place for neighbors. The circle hosted birthday celebrations, Halloween parades, and casual sports games. It was intergenerational, too. Neighbors ranged from families with newborns, like ours, to couples in their 60s. We knew each other's stories, not just names.

Sociologists refer to these community bonds as "social capital." Such networks of relationships among people help the community function effectively. In such an environment, you don't just care about your own kids. You care about your neighbors' kids. You care about the kids at your school, no matter where they reside. Your circle of interest expands beyond your home to your street, to your neighborhood, to your town or city. These relationships can help provide a sense of pride in your community and create opportunities to serve within it. This dynamic can organically create an informal exchange of services like providing car rides, childcare, and pet care.

Neighborhood design has an impact. Sidewalks elevate walkability. Protected bike lanes encourage biking for people of all ages, abilities, and speeds. The density of housing enables closer proximity of people, making it simpler to connect with others. Strong schools create a draw for families, and their proximity to home makes it easier to get involved. Neighborhood schools can be an opportunity for older residents to volunteer with youth.

Community spaces can make a difference, too. The prevalence of "third places" where people congregate has been shown to make an impact, including increasing trust, decreasing loneliness, and creating a greater sense of attachment to where we live.[41] After the first and second places of home and work, the third place is an alternate location to spend leisure time.[42] Examples of third places are parks, libraries, coffee shops, places of worship, community pools, or local watering holes. Density of third places—notably, eateries—has been shown to improve cognitive functioning.[43] Having a third place significantly influences perceived social connectedness, even if one doesn't use them regularly. Third places can be particularly useful in bringing together people of all ages. More than 90% believe that intergenerational activities, such as those at third places, help reduce loneliness across all ages, drastically cutting down the prevalence and harmful effects of loneliness.[44]

The immediate environment around home can also affect well-being. One study found a link between living near major roads and an increased risk of neurological diseases, including dementia, Parkinson's, Alzheimer's, and multiple sclerosis.[45] These conditions are believed to be caused by excessive exposure to air pollution and the incessant noise of vehicles.

The pervading culture and climate of place also affect well-being. Certain states are more beneficial for health. Take Colorado, for example, where more than 25% of the population meets the weekly recommended levels of aerobic and muscle-strengthening exercise, all living in a climate and terrain that are conducive to year-round physical activity.[46] An active culture nudges people toward physical activity. We are more likely to be active if those around us are active, and those around us are more active if the environment is conducive to such activity.

The reverse is true as well. It's harder to be active when those around you are not and the environment is less conducive to physical activity. Mississippi, Tennessee, and West Virginia are among the least active states, each with less than 15% of the population meeting the weekly recommended levels of aerobic and muscle-strengthening exercise.

Seventh-Day Adventists in Southern California live about a decade longer than other Americans.[47] The reasons are myriad—they eat healthily, are active, and have a sense of purpose through their faith. They also have a sense of belonging through their religious community. This connection to a larger group with similar values provides social connection and civic engagement.

Physical design elements of housing can also be critical, especially for older adults. One-third of older adults fall each year, which can lead to emergency room visits and hospitalizations, costing billions of dollars annually.[48] Design in bathrooms, in particular, with slip-resistant tiles, no or limited shower step entries, and grab bars can minimize risk and be deployed attractively. Unfortunately, only 3.8% of all housing units in the country are suitable for people with moderate mobility difficulties.[49]

Place has a role in financial well-being. There can be a tension between maximizing the opportunity to continue to work to produce income and taking measures to minimize annual costs. On the one hand, living in a place with a dynamic and growing economy offers the prospect of additional years of work. On the other hand, places of growing economic opportunity often have a high cost of living. Moving to a place with a low cost of living, a common consideration for those entering retirement, helps with managing annual expenditures, but a move too early may compromise the ability to work longer and gain additional income. This trade-off is particularly tricky when people are living longer and working past traditional retirement. The trend toward remote work, accelerated by the coronavirus pandemic, may alleviate some of this dilemma.

Homes can be a significant source of wealth or asset appreciation. However, houses, especially old ones, are expensive to maintain.

They are subject to unexpected or substantial one-time costs like the replacement of a roof. They may be inefficient to heat and cool or costly for insurance and real estate taxes. People tend to overlook the opportunity cost of equity in their homes that could be reinvested elsewhere for a higher return. And for those concerned about managing downside risk, selling a home at an attractive price in a timely manner can be a challenge, particularly during recessions. For these reasons, the calculus of understanding the value and cost of owning a home can be complicated but important, particularly in the context of a 100-year life.

PULLING IT ALL TOGETHER

Purpose, social connection, physical well-being, financial well-being, and place each play a key role in influencing one's life, health, and wealth spans. But it is even more powerful when these factors work in combination. For example, when exercising with friends, one benefits not just from the physical exertion but also from the social connection. Or with purposeful work, one can gain meaning by helping others or by working on an important cause, while also incrementally improving financial well-being. In the case of place, a single-family house modified to minimize falls and located amidst a robust intergenerational neighborhood provides safety and opportunities for stronger social connection.

This is part of the power of place. The right place has value in and of itself. The right home provides a level of comfort and emotional benefit, on top of positively affecting each element of well-being. In other words, getting place right has the potential to elevate life across many dimensions, while the wrong place can inhibit our well-being and happiness.

CHAPTER 2

EVALUATING WHETHER YOU ARE IN THE RIGHT PLACE

In my consulting practice, I advise leaders on strategies to grow their organizations. The first step is to gain clarity on the state of the organization. We combine data analysis with in-depth discussion to understand where the organization is in its journey. We can't provide good direction on where to go unless we know where we are at the start. This approach takes effort.

The same process is required for individuals to sort out their best path for healthy aging. The initial step is to reflect on where you are. This is not an exact science. You are likely to rely more on intuition than data, but be a hard and honest evaluator. If you don't make the effort to understand the gap between where you are and where you would like to be, you are less likely to make a change for the better.

STEP #1. CREATE A PERSONAL HEALTHY AGING DASHBOARD

The first step is to determine where you stand in key areas of healthy aging: purpose, social connection, physical well-being, financial well-being, and place.

Personal Dashboard

Purpose	0				FULL
Social Connection	0				FULL
Physical Well-Being	0				FULL
Financial Well-Being	0				FULL
Place	0				FULL

Some questions to consider include:

- For **Purpose**
  - Do you have something that gives you meaning each day? Examples can include family, work, volunteering, and faith.
  - How does your sense of purpose in these areas prompt you to make a difference beyond yourself?

- For **Social Connection**
  - Do you have a set of close relationships with persons with whom you can share important things?
  - Do these relationships extend beyond a spouse or partner?
  - Do you have family living physically close to you?
  - Do you have casual friends that you simply enjoy spending time with?
  - Do you have friends that live close by, and do you see them regularly (at least once per week) in person?
  - Do you know your neighbors? If so, do you see them, even if in passing, at least once a week?
  - Do you find yourself physically isolated to the point where you rarely see people?
  - Do you participate in any activities that routinely bring you together with a set of people?

- For **Physical Well-Being**:
  - Are you physically active in some fashion at least two times per week?

- Do you do a mix of aerobic, interval, and resistance training?
- Do you exercise with friends?
- Do you maintain a healthy diet that includes a mix of whole grains, fruit, vegetables, and fish?
- Do you smoke? Is your alcohol consumption moderate or less, such as one drink per day for women and no more than two drinks per day for men?
- Are you able to get enough quality sleep for your age and stage in life?

- For Financial **Well-Being**:
  - Do you have a financial plan for a long life, as long as 100 years, that includes goals and has sensitivities to changes in annual income, expenditures and investment returns?
  - Do you utilize third-party help, such as a financial advisor or skilled friend, to assess the quality of your plan?
  - Does your income stream compare favorably to expenses?
  - Do you have resources, including family, that could help should a need arise beyond your financial means?
  - Do you have friends or family that may need financial assistance from you?

- For **Place**:
  - Do you love where you live? Do you feel at ease in your home?
  - Does your place make it easier to cultivate and fulfill purpose?
  - Does your place facilitate social connection? Does it make it easy to see existing friends and meet new ones?
  - Does your place encourage physical well-being? Do you live in an environment where physical well-being is part of the broader culture?
  - Does your place enhance your financial well-being? Does it help you manage a favorable mix of income and expenses?

- ○ Is your home more than you can handle from a maintenance perspective?
- ○ If you or your partner has mobility constraints, is your home set up accordingly?
- ○ If you or your partner has health challenges, can your place properly accommodate them?

A couple of blank dashboards are included in the appendix to this book. One is intended for you, and the other for a partner.

For each of these areas, use the dashboard to sketch how you feel. If you feel strong in a category, that's fantastic. Fill it to three bars or more. If you feel low in an area, that's just as important to document. Fill in two bars or less. Getting a perspective of where you stand will show what areas to focus on.

While the dashboard is a self-assessment, it can be helpful to solicit input from friends or family. A spouse can be particularly insightful. Have a casual conversation with a friend, or send them a note requesting feedback. Another approach is to complete the self-evaluation exercise with a group of friends. You can talk about elements as a group, fill in self-evaluations individually, and discuss each person's response as a group. Be sure to have fun with it—such a conversation could happen over dinner or a social hour.

The process of self-evaluation can be easier said than done. As helpful as feedback from others can be, change ultimately must be driven by the individual. And it can be complicated for couples. Some areas may require significant collaboration, such as in areas of financial well-being and place. It is best for self-reflection to occur independently at first and jointly afterward. This exercise can be an opportunity for each partner to not only better appreciate their individual perspective but to also express it clearly to their partner. This conversation may lead to some aha moments. It can be a challenge for singles, as well. Particularly for those who have recently divorced or lost a partner, emotions may not allow for an accurate assessment. It's best to fill out the dashboard regardless, but recognize that the circumstances will dictate your answers.

Self-awareness is important for this exercise. Try to identify impediments from thinking openly and accurately. For example, perhaps there is a cultural and familial expectation that you will stay in the hometown or region where you raised your family. If this is not your preference, don't be afraid to reflect this reality in your rating for place. You shouldn't feel bound by cultural expectations or those set by friends and family.

Individual preferences are important to consider, even for couples. Suppose one partner visits with friends four days a week. This level of social interaction may be insufficient for an extrovert, but too much for an introvert. For each category, measure your state relative to what you want it to be. Some personality tools, such as the Myers-Briggs Type Indicator (MBTI) and the Enneagram of Personality, may help provide insights on your personality type.

Age and ability adjust your score. If you used to run marathons but are now limited to long, fast walks, that's fine. Even light activity pursued regularly could warrant a high ranking. You are not comparing yourself to yesterday; instead, you are evaluating yourself on what is possible today.

EXAMPLES OF HEALTHY AGING STRATEGIES INCORPORATING PLACE

Below are a handful of hypothetical examples to highlight the potential impact of lifestyle interventions to elevate well-being. Note that each of these examples involves a change or modification to place. These examples represent a range of scenarios—from couples in their 50s to solo agers in their 70s to adult children working with a loved one to create a plan—with the hope that at least one of them will resonate with you. Keep these names and situations in mind as you progress through the book, as they will be referenced at different points throughout.

Example #1. Mike and Lisa: Changing Place

Mike and Lisa are in their late 50s and recently became empty nesters. Married for 25 years, they have lived in Buffalo for more than a decade, and both have corporate jobs. With substantial savings and corporate pensions, they are in good shape financially. Their purpose has largely come from family and work. Nearing retirement and with children launched, purpose is an open question. While they have friends in Buffalo, they do not have a sense of rootedness compelling them to stay in the area. They are physically active—both play tennis—and feel a warmer climate would enable them to be active year-round. Their single-family house is charming but in need of frequent maintenance and is too large for their needs.

After careful planning and coordination, they decide to make a big change. They relocate to a suburb of Dallas. They purchase a smaller house with manageable costs in an age-restricted community. Mike starts a part-time consulting practice serving not-for-profit clients, and Sue volunteers in the greater community. They reach out to peers in the neighborhood and create a social network. They use their extra time and warmer weather to be more physically active.

In the end, through a set of significant decisions, they are able to elevate two low areas—purpose and place—and turn them into strengths. They improve their physical well-being with a more active lifestyle and social connection by establishing relationships in their neighborhood and the greater community.

Before

Purpose	0	FULL
Social Connection	0	FULL
Physical Well-Being	0	FULL
Financial Well-Being	0	FULL
Place	0	FULL

After

Purpose	0	FULL
Social Connection	0	FULL
Physical Well-Being	0	FULL
Financial Well-Being	0	FULL
Place	0	FULL

Example #2. Krishna and Mamta: Finding Community

Krishna and Mamta are empty nesters in their 60s and live in suburban Houston. Krishna enjoys working as an accountant but would like to scale back to part-time work by starting his own practice. Mamta is a nurse at a local hospital. They both find purpose from their jobs, but their work schedules crowd out time for exercise. Cooking for two can get tiresome, so they often don't eat healthily. They are in fine financial shape but must continue to work and watch their expenses. Their current home was chosen based on its proximity to good public schools. They are friendly but not close with neighbors. They would like to live close to their friends in the Indian community. If they could "rightsize" to a smaller home in line with their current needs and be closer to their good friends, then a change of place could considerably improve their well-being. Being part of an intergenerational community is a priority for them.

Krishna and Mamta decide to make a change. They find a two-story townhome elsewhere in Houston adjacent to close friends and near others in the Indian community. Their social life changes as they spend more time with friends. Their location is walkable to stores and restaurants. They get involved in the Indian community, including mentoring young parents. The townhome includes various universal design features, including a walk-in shower and slip-resistant tiles in the master bathroom, and there is an option to add an elevator in the future. Universal design is a design philosophy aimed at creating spaces that can appeal to a broad range of people, including those with mobility limitations. By having these features, there is the prospect that their townhome can support their future needs. The home also has an office for Krishna should he decide to shift to part-time work at home. Now, they are in a position to age proximate to their close friends for years to come. Their decision to change places dramatically improves social connection while also elevating sense of purpose, physical well-being, and place.

Before

Purpose	0 [▨▨▨▨▨▨░░░░░░░]	FULL
Social Connection	0 [▨▨▨░░░░░░░░░░]	FULL
Physical Well-Being	0 [▨▨▨▨░░░░░░░░]	FULL
Financial Well-Being	0 [▨▨▨▨▨▨░░░░░░]	FULL
Place	0 [▨▨▨▨▨▨░░░░░░]	FULL

After

Purpose	0 [▨▨▨▨▨▨▨▨▨▨░░]	FULL
Social Connection	0 [▨▨▨▨▨▨▨▨▨▨▨▨]	FULL
Physical Well-Being	0 [▨▨▨▨▨▨░░░░░░]	FULL
Financial Well-Being	0 [▨▨▨▨▨▨▨░░░░░]	FULL
Place	0 [▨▨▨▨▨▨▨▨▨░░░]	FULL

Example #3. Robert and Lucinda: Following Family

Robert and Lucinda have lived in suburban New Jersey for too long. They are tired of traffic and high taxes. What once felt like home is no longer the case. Even though they have friends, social connections have weakened. Robert recently retired from a career in the pharmaceutical industry and consults on the side. Lucinda is a retired schoolteacher. They have savings but can't afford to live lavishly. They exercise and watch their diet, but in recent years, they have felt uninspired. They are in their early 70s and in a rut. Their only child, a daughter, lives in Seattle, is married, and just had a baby. They would like to be involved in the life of their grandchild. They are itching for a change.

Robert and Lucinda make a big change: they sell their house and relocate to Seattle. They decide to rent an apartment within a short walk of their daughter's house. While apartment rent is high, all-in housing costs are more predictable and less expensive as compared to their prior house. Getting used to a small space is hard at first, but they adjust. They are initially concerned about safety in a city but find their fears are unfounded. They enjoy the convenience and pleasures of urban living, a contrast to their prior life in the suburbs. The healthy culture of the Northwest rubs off on them, and they are consistently on the go and eat healthily. The apartment building they select, while not age restricted, has an abundance of active older residents, and they are welcomed into the social scene. They regularly see their daughter's family and play an active role in their granddaughter's life. The transition is not without difficulty and stress, particularly in the effort to downsize, but they believe the reward is worth it.

Their decision to change places dramatically improves purpose, social connection, and place while also raising physical well-being and financial well-being. They recognize the risk that her daughter's family may move from Seattle, but pledge to consider their options if and when this circumstance arises. It is the right thing for now.

Before

Purpose	0	FULL
Social Connection	0	FULL
Physical Well-Being	0	FULL
Financial Well-Being	0	FULL
Place	0	FULL

After

Purpose	0	FULL
Social Connection	0	FULL
Physical Well-Being	0	FULL
Financial Well-Being	0	FULL
Place	0	FULL

Example #4. Gail: Moving into a Retirement Community

In her mid-70s, Gail is a solo ager: an older adult without children. She is also a recent widow. She lives in a two-story single-family house in the suburbs of Minneapolis. She loves the Midwest—she was born and raised in Minnesota—and can't imagine living elsewhere. She loves her neighborhood and church, but since her husband passed away, she has grown distant from friends. She has found it hard socially to be single amidst couples, and she has no desire to remarry. She retired from a career leading nonprofit organizations and remains involved in the greater community. Her savings are limited, but she owns her home with no mortgage. She's active during the nonwinter months, but her life slows down during the cold months. She's lost motivation to cook and relies on prepared meals and takeout. Though healthy, Gail is concerned about what may happen when her health fades.

Gail decides to sell her house and move into a senior living community. Working closely with her financial advisor, she researches options and finds one she can afford that has the sense of community she craves. It is a life plan community where all levels of care are provided, and her financial resources are sufficient. The transition is a challenge as she leaves a home she loves. But she quickly connects with residents, especially single women. She joins a Bible study and forges deep friendships. She is grateful to make new friends and enjoys the daily opportunities to socialize. While she is one of the youngest members of the community, she is glad she moved while still in good health. It was the right time, and her energy has helped her engage in the community. She stays connected to her volunteering activities in the greater community and attends her church.

Her move to a senior living community significantly improved her social connection and physical well-being while modestly improving her financial well-being, as she now has a viable plan for when her health fades. Place ranks the same, as she traded a house she loved but was difficult to maintain for an environment that is small but requires little upkeep.

Before

Purpose	0 ▓▓▓▓▓▓▓░░░░░░░	FULL
Social Connection	0 ▓▓▓░░░░░░░░░░░	FULL
Physical Well-Being	0 ▓▓▓░░░░░░░░░░░	FULL
Financial Well-Being	0 ▓▓░░░░░░░░░░░░	FULL
Place	0 ▓▓▓▓▓▓░░░░░░░	FULL

After

Purpose	0 ▓▓▓▓▓░░░░░░░░	FULL
Social Connection	0 ▓▓▓▓▓▓▓░░░░░	FULL
Physical Well-Being	0 ▓▓▓▓▓▓▓▓▓░░░	FULL
Financial Well-Being	0 ▓▓▓▓░░░░░░░░	FULL
Place	0 ▓▓▓▓▓▓░░░░░░░	FULL

Example #5. Bob: Staying Put

Bob is in his late 70s, and he loves his place. He lives in a single-family, ranch-style house in Southern California. It has been his home for decades. He is divorced and has three children, two of whom live within an hour's drive. He has friends, though in recent years he has been seeing them less. Health issues are increasingly a challenge among his peers, and good friends have passed away. He doesn't ex-ercise—most of his activity is tending to his garden—and he drinks more than he should. He is fully retired and has no clear purpose. He is agitated about the future of the country but doesn't do anything about it except share dystopian posts on Facebook. He is in reasonable financial shape, but if his health deteriorates, he will not be able to afford long-term care without selling his home or utilizing a reverse mortgage. His children are concerned about social isolation and its impact on his health. The pandemic reinvigorated his desire to remain in his house as he ages; he loathes the idea of living in a retirement community, particularly if there is a risk of being quarantined in a small apartment.

Bob decides to stay put. With the urging of his children, however, he develops a plan. He adds an accessible dwelling unit (ADU) in the back of his property. This ADU is designed for one person and includes universal design features, such as wider doorways and no stairs. It is a place where he could live when his health fades. His children pay for its construction, and he rents it to a young professional. Building the ADU creates options: he can rent the ADU and live in the house, rent the house and live in the ADU, or rent both to help pay for long-term care elsewhere. But this approach does not help other areas of his life.

Bob's actions improve financial well-being and place. He now has a more viable plan to remain in his home. He remains without purpose, however, and social connection and physical well-being are likely to worsen. Bob knows he should change and reach out to more people, but realistically he won't. Ditto for his physical well-being. He is set in his ways. His children remain concerned about his well-being and recognize that they may need to intervene and support him at a moment's notice.

Before

Purpose	0	FULL
Social Connection	0	FULL
Physical Well-Being	0	FULL
Financial Well-Being	0	FULL
Place	0	FULL

After

Purpose	0	FULL
Social Connection	0	FULL
Physical Well-Being	0	FULL
Financial Well-Being	0	FULL
Place	0	FULL

STEP #2. MAKING A PLAN FOR CHANGE

In each hypothetical situation, at least some element of well-being was low. While it requires effort to self-assess the situation, it takes more energy to take action. Some situations, like Robert and Lucinda's relocation from New Jersey to Seattle, involve significant change. Others, like Bob's decision to stay put, require modest changes. Changes to place tend to be significant.

Change of any kind is hard, particularly later in life. The adage "everyone wants progress but no one wants change" often rings true. There must be sufficient interest, determination, resources, and support to overcome the inertia required to change, even if the need for change is obvious and necessary. In the case of couples, it requires strong communication and coordination. For singles, reaching out to others for support and encouragement is critical. Few of us will change as quickly and significantly as we should. And that's okay. We should give ourselves a measure of grace and recognize that even a small step in the right direction is better than no step.

As you look at your dashboard, ask yourself in what area you might start. Research has shown that it is important to develop a plan, not just indicate that you want to do better. Experts recommend creating SMART goals: goals that are specific, measurable, attainable, relevant, and timely. It is also helpful to identify obstacles to your achieving your goals.[1] You might consider brainstorming about these obstacles with family, friends, and experts to be fully aware of the things that can get in your way. Self-monitoring, such as logging behavior on paper or with technology, can help track your progress toward a goal. Research has shown that the process of consistently tracking one's behavior can be an intervention in and of itself. BJ Fogg, behavior scientist and director of the Behavior Design Lab at Stanford University, recommends that it is best to make tiny behavioral changes that you can commit to and build momentum toward bigger changes.[2]

Some lifestyle modifications can be made without requiring considerable energy and risk. In the area of purpose, for example, there are resources and tools readily available to assess and improve sense of purpose. A number of initiatives at universities, including Harvard's Advanced Leadership Initiative, Stanford's Distinguished Careers Institute, and the University of Minnesota's Advanced Careers Initiative, offer programs to help alumni and other interested individuals go back to school to determine what their next chapter could look like. Chip Conley, author of *Wisdom @ Work: The Making of a Modern Elder*, created the Modern Elder Academy, which offers immersive workshops in Mexico that help participants gain greater clarity on what's next. Marc Freedman founded Encore.org, an organization dedicated to help people at midlife and beyond find avenues for purpose, particularly with a socially minded focus. Freedman is passionate about helping older adults finding greater purpose in building meaningful relationships with younger people.[3] Similarly, there are dedicated resources to help identify strategies to elevate social connection, physical well-being, and financial well-being.

Changes to place, however, often require a lot of energy and resources. It can be challenging to make decisions about relocating, too, which adds an extra layer of risk. A decision to sell a house and move to a new location is more involved than hiring a personal trainer to develop a customized exercise routine. Even if you decide to stay in your current home, modifications to existing physical space can be costly, so you want to be sure you are making the right decisions. It can be valuable to find lower-risk approaches to verify that a significant change to place is the right decision.

DESIGN THINKING TO FIND YOUR PLACE

Design thinking is an iterative approach to innovation that relies on understanding users' needs, challenging assumptions, developing prototypes, and testing their effectiveness. It becomes rinse and repeat until an adequate or breakthrough solution is found. Design thinking is an approach used by many leading companies, like Apple, Google, and Samsung, and top universities. It is credited with a number of famous innovations, such as the computer mouse.

But these principles need not be constrained only to corporate or academic settings. Bill Burnett and Dave Evans teach students at Stanford how to apply design thinking to life decisions. They published their teachings in a book titled *Designing Your Life*, which is centered on creating a set of hypotheses and making bets—small, calculated bets—on whether what you think you're good at and enjoy is true in real-life experiences. It is a popular book among recent graduates, but it also resonates with older adults looking for their next chapter.

Design thinking can also be applied in the context of finding your place. The design thinking approach can help narrow down options that you *think* may lead to the right answer. The operative word is "think," however. The cost of a bad decision can be significant, so finding ways to move from think to know can be valuable. Design thinking suggests that you outline specific ideas or possible outcomes and then test them simply and quickly, where possible, to determine whether what you assume you would like is true. Reality often surprises us.

Examples of applying design thinking in the context of place are numerous. Let's suppose you think you want to downsize from a single-family house in the suburbs to a condominium apartment in the city. Try it without making the change first. Find a friend who has a place downtown that you could use for a weekend or a week, or search online for short-term rentals. Find something close to the location and layout that you desire. Try it, and take careful notes about your experience and how it differed from expectations. Consider which parts are changeable and which are not. If you are not satisfied but want to learn more, try it again, making the necessary tweaks to provide better insights around areas of concern. For example, if you thought you could live in 1,200 square feet but found it too small, identify a larger space that you think could work better but is still in your budget.

This approach can be particularly important when the degree of change is large. For example, evaluating retirement communities, especially those that involve a significant upfront payment, can be a great use of design thinking principles. Stay in a model apartment for a few days. Experience the community, including meals and social gatherings. Make the experience as normal or as close to how your life would look if you were to move in. In our hypothetical examples above, Bob could have done a short stay at a retirement community to see if the realities matched his fears prior to making the decision and subsequent investment to stay put.

Design thinking can be helpful when one partner is more skeptical of change than another. Have the skeptical partner identify concerns about a move, and link them to a particular option. Then, create a test that specifically addresses those concerns to see if they hold. Going back to our example of a move to a retirement community, suppose the skeptical partner is concerned the community's culture is too insular and the residents uninteresting. By spending a few days and nights at the retirement community, these concerns can be addressed head-on to determine their validity.

Possible moves to other regions of the country are also candidates for design thinking. My friends Payton and Grant unwittingly applied design thinking principles in their eventual move from San Francisco to Richmond, Virginia. They loved San Francisco but were discouraged by the cost of living and missed family on the opposite coast. They launched a multiyear process exploring specific cities on the East Coast, using vacations and business trips to get a firsthand look. They created a short list of locales where they could imagine their family thriving while also being a great place for when they become empty nesters. In the end, they chose Richmond, where Grant subsequently found a job that aligned with his skills.

SELF-EVALUATION IS NOT A ONE-TIME THING AND TAKING THE NEXT STEP

Just as it is hard to make a change without assessing why change is necessary, it is important to appreciate that evaluating your situation is not a one-and-done proposition. Circumstances shift, with some requiring a change to ensure our well-being.

Some transitions are obvious: end of a primary work career, divorce, loss of a spouse, change in physical or cognitive condition, significant financial loss. But most shifts are small and almost imperceptible. Maybe it is finding less meaning in activities and relationships that previously provided it. Maybe it is not seeing a good friend as often, prompting a sense of loneliness. Maybe it is falling out of a pattern of regular exercise and healthy eating. Perhaps you realize your financial situation is not as strong as you thought. Perhaps you don't feel as emotionally connected to your home.

In each situation, it is important to take a moment and do an inventory check. Update your dashboard. How am I feeling about my circumstances, and does it necessitate a change in my life? If you don't perform such a check and make changes when necessary, the risk of abrupt changes happening to you increases. In other words, there can be a window of opportunity for proactive change. If this opportunity is not taken, change is more likely to be reactive.

Consider the example with Gail, the solo ager who moved to a retirement community. She assessed her situation and found that she was low in social engagement and physical well-being. This evaluation triggered a response by moving into a retirement community suited to her tastes. This is a proactive change.

Gail's situation could have looked much different. She could have not taken the effort to evaluate her situation or chose to ignore the results from her self-evaluation. Her social disconnectedness and decreasing physical well-being would have been her reality regardless. At some point, something would happen. Significant health issues would likely present themselves stemming from loneliness, social isolation, or a lack of physical exercise. It could be a heart attack, stroke, or a fall where she breaks her hip. Under any of these circumstances, a change is needed, but it is reactive, urgent, and stressful.

Adult children and close friends play an important role. Think of the dashboard as you interact with a loved one, and assess whether a key dimension of well-being is being neglected. Think of Bob's situation and the influence of his children to prompt him to make a plan leading to the addition of an ADU.

The rest of this book is focused on how to consider potential changes to place. It looks at considerations from evaluating metropolitan areas to determining the impact of neighborhoods and community. It details specific types of dwellings ranging from single-family homes to apartments, from age-restricted housing to senior living to emerging models. It looks at how home is likely to change with technology and evolve to become the centerpiece of health and health care delivery.

Part V, Taking Action, provides an opportunity to revisit your self-evaluation. While the current chapter prompts you to evaluate your well-being, the final part of the book prompts you to consider changes to improve well-being with place as a key consideration. It offers specific action steps, whether you decide to make the best of your current place or launch a process of finding a new place and making it work.

But first, let's tackle one of the great misperceptions of aging: the viability of aging in place.

CHAPTER 3

MOVING FROM AGING IN PLACE TO LIVING IN COMMUNITY

We are creatures of habit. We like what's comfortable. We have our favorite coffee shops and restaurants. We like to be known. In a world of constant change, it's nice when people know your name and you know theirs. Recall the lyrics from the theme song of the sitcom *Cheers*: "You want to be where everybody knows your name." Developing this comfort takes time—years in most cases.

It should come as no surprise that the majority of older people—about 75%—wish to age in place.[1] "Aging in place" typically means living in your existing home for as long as possible; hopefully forever. For most older adults who own a home, this means a single-family house in the suburbs and could ultimately translate to living in one home for decades.[2]

My parents are a good example. They are in their mid-70s and have lived in their single-family house for almost 40 years. They have a strong social network and work in the area. Plus, their house is a single-level, ranch-style house on a flat lot with few stairs, and thus conducive to aging in place.

Living in one home for so long can make a change challenging. For one, there are strong emotional ties. My parents' house has been a place where their children were raised, where grandchildren visited, and where countless celebrations and keystone memories were held.

But there are also practical considerations. My parents have accumulated stuff over the years. A lot of stuff. The sheer size of it all makes the idea of moving feel overwhelming.

For my parents and no doubt millions of others, their plan is to age in place. For some, this decision is intentional. I suspect for most it is the default plan. *It's the plan in absence of a plan.*

Before diving into the merits and drawbacks of this approach, it is important to acknowledge that "aging in place" is an awful term. It suggests that getting older is passive—something that is happening *to* us as opposed to something we have some influence over. It also implies that people are static, like statues. It is as if older people are superglued in place. It's ironic because we know that central to healthy aging is being active. At a minimum, a better term is needed.[3]

MERITS OF AGING IN PLACE

Aging in place has significant advantages. First of all, it maintains the status quo. The psychological and emotional ties to home are not severed. This strategy allows one to maintain existing networks of friendships, continue attending familiar places of worship, and stay connected to health care providers. As part of aging in place, the individual maintains control of life.

There can be financial advantages, taxes being one key area. Some states and counties offer financial incentives to age in place. For example, in California, real estate taxes are based on the purchase price, not the current assessed value, and have capped annual increases. Proposition 13 established this approach in the 1970s based on the sentiment that older Californians should not be priced out of their homes. It makes a huge difference, particularly for those on a fixed income. Some municipalities, such as Montgomery County, Maryland, provide tax incentives to construct or remodel homes that accommodate a wide range of accessibility needs.

Another financial advantage is related to the capital gains tax. If a couple lives in a home and one of them dies, the home value is stepped up to the current assessed value for capital gains purposes. For homeowners that have experienced significant real estate appreciation in their properties, this is a major benefit, particularly for the financial stability of the remaining spouse or heirs of the estate.

Aging in place can be less expensive more broadly as well. Senior living settings are expensive, as chapter 9 details, and any effort to delay or avoid institutional care will save money. Even if care is required, a home setting can also be less expensive than senior living, particularly if needs are minimal.

A decision to do something different than aging in place can be hard individually and collectively. It's often difficult for an individual to make a big change, but it can be even more challenging for couples. When spouses have differing views on preference for place, it can create tension or, worse, an impasse. It can be easier to delay a big decision until one must be made, typically triggered by pressing health or financial considerations.

MAKING AGING IN PLACE EASIER

Whether a decision to age in place has been explicitly made or not, a number of trends are making this option more feasible. Home modification is often an important but complicated step. Fortunately, there is an increasing number of specialists to help modify homes to support aging in place. Certified Aging-in-Place Specialists (CAPS) are uniquely trained to make appropriate home modifications. This includes elements such as additional task lighting, zero-entry walkways, grab bars, and other home modifications. If done well, these changes can strengthen home as a place of personal and social meaning as well as improve safety and comfort.[4] Utilizing experienced specialists in design and execution can ensure that the right changes are made for the long haul.

While home modification can be expensive, particularly for those on tight budgets or fixed income, advocates are pushing for subsidies to support aging in place. A typical home renovation to support aging in place costs between $10,000 and $25,000, not a small figure for middle-income consumers.[5] Louis Tennebaum, the founder and president of HomesRenewed, sees an opportunity for the federal government and health care institutions to save money by creating economic incentives to make aging in place easier. Delaying or avoiding institutional care by staying at home longer can save individuals and the government billions of dollars.

Technology and new models for health care delivery, the subject of part V of this book, are making aging in place more feasible. With the availability of technology-enabled on-demand services, such as grocery and food delivery, transportation, and home maintenance, it is easier to manage life without leaving home. Voice-enabled smart home technology provides ease of control for home security, lighting, and appliances. Consumer wearables and in-home sensors track vitals and activity and can reach out for help without human intervention. Telehealth allows patients to consult with health care professionals without leaving their home, and an increasing number of health care services can make house calls.

Communities are making it easier to age in place, too. The Village to Village Network is a group of over 240 "villages," with more than 100 developments in 41 states and the District of Columbia.[6] These independent villages are social support networks that provide necessary services such as transportation, technology assistance, and errand support, community engagement activities, and other resources to support aging in place. Members are typically charged a modest monthly fee, around $50 per month, to access to these services.

Local policymakers are better understanding how to support aging in place. The World Health Organization (WHO) leads a global effort to prepare countries and cities for aging. In partnership with WHO, AARP has created the Age-Friendly Network, which as of the end of 2020 is composed of nearly 500 communities, six states, and a territory.[7] The network encompasses nearly 100 million people, or more than one-third of the US population. Membership requires a community's elected leadership to make the town, city, county, or state a great place to live for people of all ages. Action plans include outdoor spaces, buildings, transportation, housing, health services, and more. The Milken Institute Center for the Future of Aging has put the spotlight on mayors, with nearly 200 mayors across the United States, including for many of the largest cities, signing a pledge to join the movement for purposeful, healthy aging and to create cities that are livable for all.[8]

The implication of these trends—from increasing availability of home modifications to technology-enabled products and services to health services oriented to the home to grassroots community organizations to changes in local policy—is that aging in place should be easier in the future. But a critical question remains: *Is aging in place really what we want?*

AGING IN PLACE AS A FALLACY

Despite its allure, aging in place does not deliver on its promise. It is rarely the right strategy for the long term, particularly if one is looking to make the most of the benefits of a longer life.

The challenges are numerous. First, aging in place can simply be unrealistic. Much of our existing housing stock was not designed with an aging society in mind. Only about 3% of the housing stock *in the entire country* has two or more design elements conducive to aging.[9] Moreover, much of the single-family housing supply is located in the suburbs and is largely dependent on a car for transport. Even with on-demand transportation, it can be costly and inconvenient to get around. Most suburbs do not have sidewalks or walkways that are adequate for people with mobility constraints.

It can also be inefficient for people and services to come to you. While technology is making it easier for services to be delivered, it is still a challenge and often expensive for services to be delivered to the home, especially for health care needs. For those in need of home care, for example, hourly rates can be $20 or more, and for those with greater needs, monthly costs can be $4,000 or more.[10]

Housing itself can be expensive, too. Beyond the costs of home modifications to make a house more appropriate, there are real estate taxes, insurance, utility costs, and routine home maintenance costs to consider. One must also take note of substantial one-time home expenditures, like a new roof or a heating, ventilation, and air conditioning (HVAC) system, which can cost tens of thousands of dollars collectively.

There are also hidden costs to aging in place. The most frequent one is the opportunity cost associated with home equity. Particularly in markets with limited house appreciation, the dollars tied into the house are likely receiving a substandard return relative to investments in the broader investment market. For example, if someone has home equity of $300,000 in a stagnate housing market and the stock market yields a 7% return, this is an *annual* opportunity cost to the house owner of more than $20,000. This cost is hard to remember because there is no bill associated with it.

Perhaps it is not surprising that housing costs are an increasing burden for older adults. Harvard's Joint Center for Housing estimates that about a quarter of homeowners 65 and older are cost burdened from housing, meaning they pay 30% or more of income on housing.[11] That proportion increases with age. It makes sense: the costs associated with maintaining a home tend to increase with time, even as homeowners age and may be on a fixed income. In markets where there is home appreciation, the burden can be offset by home value and the feasibility of leveraging this value.

It can be financially risky to own a home later in life. More than three-quarters of people aged 50 and older own their home, and on average, the equity in their home represents about half of their net worth.[12] In large metro markets, especially on the coasts, home values have increased substantially in recent decades.

But what if something happens to this nest egg? What if you can't sell your home when you want to? Or, more importantly, when you need to? What if you are forced to sell for much less than what it is worth? Recessions and pandemics can make an attractive home sale anything but certain.

Risks go beyond the next economic downturn. What about climate change? I have friends along the East Coast, for example, who are con-

cerned about the impact of climate change on their homes and communities and have elected to move preemptively. They are not the only
ones. In some areas, prospective buyers are considering the impact of
climate change on coastal homes, and experts expect home values to
decline as a result in the future.[13]

What are the effects of changing buyer preferences and affordability? As the jobs of today and tomorrow collect in select cities and regions, it represents an opportunity for homeowners anchored in these
metropolitan areas to benefit from housing appreciation and liquidity.
For geographic areas that do not see growth, the risk associated with
homeownership increases.

I saw this up close on a family trip to Pittsburgh, Pennsylvania. My
dad is from the area, and while we were visiting we toured his child-
hood neighborhood. The city is thriving. Technology companies have
put down roots. Health care and financial institutions are also strong
draws. As a result, graduates of the leading local universities, such as
Carnegie Mellon, University of Pittsburgh, and Chatham University,
are staying after graduation. Just a decade or so ago, young people left
the city in record numbers. Real estate development is active amidst
rising home prices and home sales.

But the trajectory of Marienville, Pennsylvania, the rural town of
my dad's family's old hunting cabin, is different. The area is two hours
from downtown Pittsburgh, but it might as well be on a different plan-
et. As the popularity of hunting has faded in this area, so has the town.
For-sale signs were aplenty; potential buyers not so much. I spoke to a
waitress serving us lunch to learn more about what changed in the past
25 years, about the time since I last visited. For a variety of reasons, the
town has contracted; she said the elementary school, for example, has
half the number of students from its peak. Those who could get out of
town did. Those remaining are stuck in place.

While aging in place faces practical challenges and economic considerations, the biggest risk associated is the possibility of social isolation, which can be highly detrimental to health. Simply put, a home
that at one time represented comfort and connection with friends and

family can become a place of solitary confinement and loneliness. Environments change in relation to our needs and abilities. What was great for a young family may be a challenge for older adults without the built-in social networks that schools and kids' activities provide. Turnover in a neighborhood also affects social networks. About half of older adults don't know *any* of their current neighbors.[14]

It takes effort to stay engaged in our community. If we don't stay connected, ties naturally break. The result is that we can become physically and socially isolated from others. Our address may stay the same, but our experience in our home may be vastly different. So, if one's goal is to thrive with age, aging in place—often experienced as staying in the same detached single-family home in the suburbs for decades—may not be the best path forward.

MOVING TO A BETTER FRAMEWORK:
LIVING IN COMMUNITY

It is time for a new paradigm. Rather than aging in place, more should aspire to live in community. "Living in community" has several advantages.

First, it swaps the passive word "aging" for the active word "living." It connotes an intentional effort to make the most of one's current life stage. In essence, we are both "aging" and "living" at the same time, but we can choose to be more proactive about its role in the context of having a finite amount of time on earth. Living suggests an opportunity to soak up every moment, while aging suggests that we are passively waiting to die. How awful is that?

Second, it exchanges "place" for "community." While place has technically a broader definition, most think of place in this context as one's current home. Community has a dual meaning, however. It decouples your residence from the broader community at large. It opens the opportunity to live in places that may be different than your current single-family residence yet still be in the same geographic area. It allows for scenarios that are more practical, financially prudent, and socially uplifting.

The other benefit of the word community is that it highlights what is needed to thrive: others. It doesn't mean that we need to be around people 24-7—a frightening thought, especially for introverts—but we know that constantly being alone is awful. The lack of face-to-face contact on top of the burden of aging leads to undue stress. We are best to embrace the definition of community provided by Charles Vogl, author of *The Art of Community*, as a "group of individuals who share a mutual concern for one another's welfare."[15]

Living in community is happening today. One example is our neighbor Colette. She is a widow in her mid-80s and has lived in her home for decades. Her detached single-family house has some design advantages—the key one is that it is one story. She regularly does yoga—even teaches a class—and makes time for daily meditation. She regularly volunteers in the community, as she has for decades. She knows her neighbors. Her family is in the area and active in her life. In fact, she's the primary caregiver and health advocate for her daughter, who is fighting cancer. She may live alone, but she is not lonely. When we need help, she's our first call. Technically, she may fit the traditional aging in place definition, but she's living in community.

My friends the Grottons, a lovely couple in their 70s, are another example. They moved into an apartment building I co-developed in Rockville, Maryland, a suburb of Washington, DC, called The Stories at Congressional Plaza. This community is unique in the area, as it incorporates universal design features such as wider doorways, slip-resistant tiles in the bathroom, and blocking to easily add grab bars. The Stories has staff that help coordinate lifestyle and health services and a culture that encourages socializing through regular programming. A key element of this development is that it is open to all ages and flexible to support people with a variety of needs.

The Grottons embraced the concept. Since downsizing from a single-family house to move closer to family, they have elected to live in an apartment. They appreciate the financial benefits of renting, including lower costs and financial flexibility. They also like to get to know their neighbors and make new friends. They host a monthly game and crafts night for people in the apartment community, which attract people of all ages. They are also part of a group that hosts occasional potlucks.

Collette and the Grottons are examples that stand in contrast to a former neighbor growing up, Carlotta. She was brilliant and perhaps the most well-read person I had ever met. Single and never married, she had ample time to read over the years, but over time, she became a recluse. My family might have been the only people on our block who knew her name. My sister and I would visit for chats with her, sometimes bringing food. Ultimately, her health deteriorated. Her only regular human contact came from her caregiver. She likely would have been better served in an environment where she could have maintained her personal space, including her books, yet continue to be connected to others and have access to services. I believe physical isolation precipitated her health decline, and her place—its location and design—made the provision of services more expensive and less efficient than it could have been otherwise.

Sadly, stories like Carlotta's are not unusual. Bob's decision to stay put in his home (see chapter 2) may lead to a similar outcome. Aging in place works until it doesn't. We can do better. In fact, as a society, we have done better.

The practice of living in community—using place to thrive in the age of longevity—is not new. It's how things were for thousands of years. What's different now is that living in community doesn't naturally happen. We need to cultivate it.

PART II

WHERE IS THE RIGHT PLACE FOR YOU?

Part II explores the various options for place, with considerations for regions, metropolitan areas, and neighborhoods.

CHAPTER 4

REGIONS, STATES, AND METRO AREAS

I studied engineering in college, but I almost got weeded out along the way. Physics 103 nearly took me down. It was an infamous class, known as a litmus test for whether you had what it took to make it through engineering school. It separated the wheat from the chaff, and I took it seriously. But it was almost all for naught, thanks to the final exam. The exam mattered a lot, accounting for 75% of the final grade. I felt comfortable until the final question, but these professors were cruel. The problem took half a page to explain. It was something about a ball falling from a ledge and then making its way through a maze and falling into water and who knows what. The killer thing was that the problem had no numbers. Every potential value was expressed as a Greek letter. It used all 24 letters of the Greek alphabet. I was lost in its complexity. It was literally all Greek to me. I did my best to craft a solution, but I didn't make much progress. I prayed for partial credit.

Trying to find the right place to live can feel like the trauma of the Physics 103 final exam. It's easy to get overwhelmed by the complexity. There are so many variables to consider. And the proper weight for each one is subjective. It's even more complicated when making decisions as a couple, as you may not value each variable equally.

As we've established, however, where you live matters, and it's important to wade through the Greek alphabet of options to find the best solution. Objectively, some variables matter more than others. For example, what part of the country—specifically which region, state, and greater metropolitan market—can have a profound influence on well-being.

BROAD DEFINITION OF HOME

When evaluating place, we need to make sure that our definition of home is broad. Home is not just our immediate physical space. Our home is a composite of our country, region, state, metropolitan area, neighborhood, and physical dwelling. There are myriad options and factors to consider within each of these dimensions.

PHYSICAL ELEMENTS THAT COMPRISE HOME

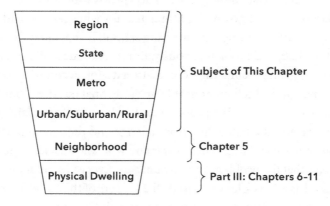

Each layer in this composite matters. For example, you can live in an amazing region that is growing and has a culture of health and well-being but live in a neighborhood that is unsafe with little social connection. Your lived experience will be far from optimal. The opposite can be true, too. You can live in a house and neighborhood perfect for you but within a metropolitan area that is not thriving.

Getting all of this perfect is impossible. There are too many variables in play. But the aspiration for finding the best for you is important. At the same time, you need to be realistic about change. Even if your home—broadly defined—satisfies you, circumstances change. Your preferences and needs may shift, resulting in lower satisfaction with your current home, or characteristics of place may change, such as a region beginning to struggle economically or a neighborhood becoming less safe, negatively affecting well-being. A significant shift in any area—triggered by your circumstances or changes in place—may trigger a need to reevaluate home altogether.

Home is a personal choice. There are objective measures that matter: economic opportunity, social cohesion, and safety, to name a few. But plenty of other variables come down to individual preference. Some like it hot, others don't. Some like mountains, others like the ocean. There can be a tension for each person to resolve when personal preference is at odds with what is generally best for their well-being. This tension can be seen when evaluating regions of the country to live.

REGIONAL CONSIDERATIONS

The five main regions of the United States—Northeast, Southeast, Midwest, Southwest, and West—have stereotypes. Stereotypes may have flaws, but there's an element of truth in them. People in the Northeast are intelligent and intense. The Southeast is conservative and cordial. The Midwest is down to earth. People in the Southwest treasure their independent spirit. The West is active and healthy.

Data can support some of these stereotypes. According to the Centers for Disease Control and Prevention (CDC), western states lead the way in active lifestyles, with every western state having at least 20% of its population meet its guidelines for physical activity.[1] In contrast, the Southeast and Midwest are the least active, with most of their states below the 20% threshold and some below the 15% level. Overall health is strongest in the West and the Northeast. It is decidedly worst in the Southeast, with the Southwest not far behind. Correspondingly, pedestrians and bikers are most at risk of fatal collisions in the Southeast and Southwest.[2] Education attainment, as measured by advanced degrees, is highest per capita in the Northeast.

Since 2010, population growth has concentrated in the Southeast, West, and Southwest.[3] Projections expect this growth to continue and perhaps accelerate. It is largely driven by the millennial generation, who have flocked to hubs of economic opportunity with a reasonable cost of living. Such places are disproportionately represented in the West, Southeast, and Southwest.

Given the fact that people tend to not move very often, and when they do they are much more likely to stay within their region, it is important to understand the trajectory of your current or desired region. Given that growth is not uniformly experienced across regions, and some regions are particularly well positioned for the economy of tomorrow, some regions are better set up for success than others. There is a logic for older people, such as baby boomers, to pay attention to the movements and preferences of younger generations, such as millennials and subsequent generations. Following the movements of younger generations will likely take boomers to places with dynamic economies. Conversely, if older adults are stuck in less dynamic areas, there may be challenges liquidating their house at an attractive price. This risk may outweigh the benefits of a lower cost of living.

STATE CONSIDERATIONS

States often mirror the prevailing characteristics of their respective regions, but not always. Nevada is in the West, but it is one of the least healthy states. Conversely, Minnesota is one of the healthiest states, but its Midwest region ranks closer to the national average in health.

Looking beyond health, state policy helps differentiate states. Some states are known for business-friendly practices, including lower regulation and tax rates.[4] Florida, Texas, and Wyoming tend to rank favorably. California, New Jersey, and New York, not so much. Seven states collect no personal income tax, including Alaska, Florida, Nevada, South Dakota, Texas, Washington, and Wyoming. Some of these states make up for it by levying higher-than-normal sales or property taxes. California, Minnesota, and Oregon—with New Jersey and New

York not far behind—have the highest individual marginal income tax rates. California's rate is, as of 2020, 13.3%, about one-third higher than Oregon, which has the second-highest rate of 9.9%.[5]

Tax policy can take on particular significance for older adults. Beyond personal income, sales tax, and property taxes, other areas to consider include inheritance and estate taxes, taxes on dividends and interest, and other special taxes. For those on fixed incomes, including pensions, state tax policies can be key in determining which states are best to consider.

Not to be overlooked and perhaps most important is the fiscal health of a state. Some states are in poor financial condition because of crumbling infrastructure needs and underfunded financial commitments, such as for government pensions, and insufficient annual revenues.[6] Illinois ranks as the worst state financially, with projected insufficient funds to cover short-term obligations and substantial unfunded pension liabilities. Connecticut, Kentucky, Massachusetts, and New Jersey are also weak in this measure. Florida, Nebraska, Oklahoma, South Dakota, and Tennessee, on the other hand, are among the most solvent.

Solvency matters because a weak financial position may force a state to raise revenue, such as through tax increases, cut services, or defer important capital expenditures. Such changes may make it less attractive for current residents, triggering a desire to move as well as decrease its appeal to outsiders. In either case, these changes can negatively affect growth.

My friends Mike and Johanna moved from Illinois to Utah in large part because of a combination of tax policy and fiscal health considerations. They were born and raised in the Midwest and brought up their children in the greater Chicago area, children who have settled in other regions of the country. They were increasingly concerned about the trajectory of Illinois and reached a point where their concerns outweighed the benefits. They now live in the Salt Lake City area and work remotely for their firms. They are pleased with their decision.

Some states are better situated to accommodate the needs of older adults. Accounting for affordability, access, choice, quality of care, support of caregivers, and effectiveness of transitions throughout the care continuum, Alaska, Minnesota, Oregon, Vermont, and Washington rank the highest.[7] On the opposite side of the spectrum are Alabama, Florida, Indiana, Kentucky, Mississippi, and Tennessee.

Understanding the business model, fiscal health, and accommodations for the aging population of a state is important as you consider where to live in your later years. The coronavirus pandemic was a reminder of the significance of state resources allocated to aging. The pandemic hit long-term care facilities particularly hard, and locations with few resources to battle the outbreak were most at risk.

METROPOLITAN CONSIDERATIONS

As important as a region and a state are, the decision of which metropolitan area to reside in can be more significant. This is because daily lived experience is influenced more by the policies, cultures, and norms of an immediate area.

Evaluating metropolitan areas through the lens of longevity can be complex. Fortunately, groups like AARP and the Milken Institute's Center for the Future of Aging have created valuable benchmarks and tools to determine which variables matter most when evaluating metropolitan areas. AARP's Livability Index considers seven factors: housing, neighborhood, transportation, environment, health, engagement, and opportunity.[8] Milken centers their evaluation on nine factors: community engagement, general livability, health care, wellness, financial security, education, transportation and convenience, employment, and living arrangements.[9]

While their methodologies are similar, the most recent rankings of AARP and the Milken Institute were different. The AARP Livability Index identifies San Francisco, Boston, Seattle, Denver, and Milwaukee as its top cities with populations of 500,000 and above.[10] For midsized cities with a population of between 100,000 to 500,000,[11] Madison,

Wisconsin; Arlington, Virginia; St. Paul, Minnesota; Boulder, Colorado; and Minneapolis, Minnesota, were the top cities. Top-performing small cities with populations of between 25,000 and 100,000 were Fitchburg, Wisconsin; Sheboygan, Wisconsin; La Crosse, Wisconsin; Lafayette, Colorado; and Silver Spring, Maryland.

In contrast, the Milken Institute focuses on metropolitan areas as opposed to distinct cities. Their top performers for large metropolitan areas are Provo-Orem, Utah; Madison, Wisconsin; Durham-Chapel Hill, North Carolina; Salt Lake City, Utah; and Des Moines, Iowa. The top five small metros are Iowa City, Iowa; Manhattan, Kansas; Ames, Iowa; Columbia, Missouri; and Sioux Falls, North Dakota.

Interestingly, both groups include midwestern cities as top performers. Researchers indicate that these locations have strong engagement scores. On a relative basis, these places over-index for knowing neighbors, getting involved in the community, and volunteering.

CREATING AGE-FRIENDLY ENVIRONMENTS

Beyond these rankings, AARP and the Milken Institute are helping metropolitan areas prepare for an aging demographic. The World Health Organization and AARP have created the Age-Friendly Network of nearly 500 communities nationwide set to make communities more accommodating for aging residents. This action plan requires engagement from older adults and includes areas such as outdoor spaces and buildings, transportation, housing, social participation, respect and social inclusion, civic participation and employment, communication and information, and community and health services. The Milken Institute's Mayor's Pledge encourages civic leaders to commit to purposeful, healthy aging.

Awareness of making environments more age-friendly has now entered other sectors, including health care.[12] The John A. Hartford Foundation and the Institute for Healthcare Improvement in partnership with the American Hospital Association and the Catholic Health Association of the United States have come together to create

Age-Friendly Health Systems. Their approach is to optimize value across all stakeholders: patients, families, caregivers, health care providers, and the overall system. They focus on the four M's: mobility, matters to the patient, medication, and mentation. The near-term goal is to have 20% of hospitals and health systems commit to the program.

Through my consulting practice, I have worked alongside leaders of major health systems in Montgomery County, Maryland, just outside of Washington, DC. Montgomery County is one of the wealthiest and most ethnically diverse counties in the country. In working with MedStar Health, Johns Hopkins, Holy Cross, and Adventist as part of a joint effort led by an organization called Nexus Montgomery, we coordinated better care for older adults in the community and across health systems. Our efforts involved enhanced communication among hospital professionals, emergency, and health care providers. We also provided professional education for those serving older adults in the community. We have been able to keep a greater number of older adults out of the hospital and healthy. Other health systems across the country are going through similar changes to enhance the well-being of older adults.

Areas that embrace the Age-Friendly Health Systems framework are likely to provide better outcomes for aging than areas that don't. Systemic changes can make a big difference once they take hold. It is a movement worth watching or getting involved in regardless of whether you are certain to stay in your current place or looking to relocate.

LIVABLE CITIES

One of the trends in recent decades has been a desire for greater walkability and easier access between where one lives, works, and plays. Experts call this type of living walkable urbanism, or "WalkUPs," and there are estimated to be more than 750 of these developments in the largest 30 metropolitan areas.[13] Not surprisingly, New York leads the way with the greatest number absolute number (149). Denver, Boston, Washington, DC, San Francisco, and Chicago also rank high in terms of percentage of WalkUPs. On the other end of the spectrum, Las Vegas, Phoenix, San Antonio, and Orlando are cities where Walk-UPs are least likely to be found.

The demand for walkable urbanism has been fueled by singles and childless couples attracted to the energy, convenience, and health that this lifestyle promotes. Empty nesters and single older adults are also part of this demand.

Walkable urbanism is part of a broader effort to make cities more livable. Other factors include creating complete streets whereby the right of way is designed to enable safety for all users, including pedestrians, bicyclists, motorists, and transit riders. In so doing, complete street design makes it easier to cross streets, walk to shops, bicycle to work, and for buses to run on time. Further, some municipalities are adopting Vision Zero strategies, which seek to eliminate traffic fatalities and severe injuries.[14] Cleveland Heights, Ohio; Des Moines, Iowa; and Milwaukee, Wisconsin, have all been recognized for the quality of their complete street policies. But while vehicle deaths have been on the decline, pedestrian and bicycling fatalities have increased by 53% and 36%, respectively, from 2009 to 2018.[15] Generally speaking, states in the Southeast and Southwest are most dangerous for pedestrians and bicyclists, with Florida ranked as the worst.

I have personally experienced the impact of complete streets and the Vision Zero policy. I have bicycled to work every place I have lived and found that infrastructure for and attitudes toward bicyclists matter. San Francisco offers myriad bicycling routes that are used by the recreationalist and commuter alike. This infrastructure was created through collaboration with complete street advocates and city officials. In Baltimore, however, proponents of complete streets face headwinds from a city government focused on other priorities and a culture that prioritizes cars. Each metropolitan area is somewhere on its journey to make environments more livable, but some are moving at a far faster clip than others. A silver lining of the pandemic is that some municipalities have accelerated efforts, including with complete streets initiatives, to make their urban areas more livable.

A BET ON LOCAL

At the end of the day, the success of metropolitan areas often comes down to culture and governance. Do citizens value and prioritize healthy living across the age spectrum? Are civic leaders and government officials able to drive change? A metropolitan area that has too many competing priorities, especially urgent ones like fighting crime or fixing broken schools, is unlikely to have the time and energy to focus on making the area more attractive for older adults.

Washington, DC, is an example of a city that has prioritized the needs of older adults and is taking action. Gail Kohn is Washington's Age-Friendly city coordinator and a force of nature with decades of experience in the aging field. At the mayor's direction, she convenes her peers to ensure that aging issues are woven across many departments. Gail leads DC's Age-Friendly action plan, which has three pillars: the built environment (including housing), changing attitudes about growing older, and lifelong health and security. In addition, meaningful grassroots efforts support aging throughout the metropolitan area. The DC metropolitan area has the highest concentration of senior villages in the country. Although Washington scores well in the Livability Index, there is reason for still greater optimism given the civic leadership and grassroots efforts.

Springfield, Massachusetts, a city of approximately 150,000, is another attractive place for older people.[16] Its mayor is helping to create momentum for the city and bringing together various stakeholders, from older citizens to health institutions to various not-for-profit organizations. It is the first city to complete the age-friendly trifecta by meeting the criteria for three designations: Age-Friendly City, Age-Friendly Health System, and Dementia-Friendly City. Moreover, there is broad collaboration of like-minded organizations across the city. LiveWell Springfield Coalition brings together more than 25 organizations, including Age-Friendly Springfield, Dementia-Friendly Springfield, city departments, regional transit, and health care groups. Innovation is happening; as one example, a mobile organic fresh produce market was created in the city to increase access to fresh food.

Deciding what metropolitan market to live in is a key decision—maybe the biggest decision—and it is valuable to get a sense of what the value proposition is today and how it is likely to change. Momentum to improve livability for people of all ages, like in Washington, DC, and Springfield, is an encouraging sign.

Think back to Mike and Lisa from chapter 2. Their change was moving from Buffalo to Dallas. Their decision factored in region, state, and metropolitan considerations. Their move was partially related to seeking warmer weather to pursue an active lifestyle year-round, but other factors undoubtedly came into play. Dallas has a more positive economic trajectory and, with no income tax in Texas, they retain more of their pension income and investment returns.

URBAN VS. SUBURBAN VS. RURAL

Thinking doesn't end with the choice of a metropolitan area. You have to determine where you want to live *within* the metropolitan area. This decision includes considering whether to live in the city, outside of the city, or somewhere in between.

The Case for Cities

The appeal of city living can be strong as we age. Cities are generally the most walkable, with easy access to amenities and services. The density of cities makes them efficient for services to come to you. Given the broad mix of people that cities attract, it is common to mix with people of all ages and stages. The potential to live in an intergenerational community may be greater. Talented people and entrepreneurs tend to cluster in cities, bringing with them an unmatched dynamism and intellectual stimulation. Cities tend to be the hub of innovation: a place where the best new ideas are tried and scaled. Cities are also generally strong for health care in terms of access and quality of care. Also, particularly if your skills align with the jobs of tomorrow, it is likely the best place to find employment.

Yet cities are far from perfect when looking through the aging lens. Most desirable cities are expensive, some exceedingly so. Space for living is small. Downsizing from a spacious single-family house to a cramped apartment can be a challenge, particularly for those used to hosting friends and family. Density can heighten health risks, particularly during pandemics. Living in a city around lots of people can ironically be quite lonely, especially for older adults.[17] The anonymity of city life can make it hard to build community and trust others. Safety and noise can be concerns. It can be hard to get away and connect with nature, particularly in places where parks and open spaces are not readily available. Finally, cities are often places where ageism may be most rampant. If you are not one of the younger people doing cool things, you may not be seen as relevant.

The Case for Rural Areas and Small Towns

The case for rural and small towns is the complete inverse of that for urban living. The ability to be known and connect with people is high. It is far easier to get to know people in your town given opportunities for repeated interactions. Research shows that trust among neighbors is highest for those who live in small towns.[18] The small scale of everything allows everyone to be in each other's business, which has both pros and cons. In this regard, small towns can be a boon to social connection. These areas tend to be less expensive and allow for more living space. Opportunities to connect with the outdoors and nature are bountiful. Crime tends to be lower. The peace, tranquility, and slower pace of life can be attractive. Technology has made it possible to work and receive health care services remotely.

But small towns and rural areas face struggles in the twenty-first century. While on the surface these are areas can be less expensive, they can also be on the wrong side of the supply-demand dynamic. Demographics can lean unsustainably older as younger, talented people cluster in other, more urban, areas, which can have a negative effect on the trajectory for economic growth. Finding service providers, whether for home maintenance or health care, can be difficult and expensive because demand is greater than supply, and it is more expensive to serve low-density areas. The environment is more dependent on cars, so losing the ability to drive elevates risks of social and physical isolation. Finally, access to health care can be a challenge. Even with improvements in telehealth and other technologies, rural areas and small towns have few access points for health care, and finding quality providers can be a challenge. Health emergencies can take longer to address, introducing additional health risks.

The Case for Small Cities and the Suburbs

Suburban areas and small cities offer the prospect of the best combination of urban and rural benefits. A small number of suburban locations offer high walkability to amenities and services like urban environments do. The lower density of these areas provides more of a human scale to get to know neighbors and establish human connections, more akin to living in a small town, and presents less health risk in pandemics. In addition to walkability, there can be other mobility options beyond a car. Some suburbs provide transit access to an urban core for amenities and provide more space. Suburbs and small cities can offer a wide range of housing options, from single-family homes to apartments to duplexes and more.

Suburban and small cities also bring together some unattractive elements of urban and rural. They can be isolating. With the density of families living in the suburbs, people without families can feel excluded. Most suburbs offer little walkability, and infrastructure is not designed for older adults. Given the scale of suburban sprawl, modifying existing developments can be prohibitive. Lack of density can cause some of the same problems rural environments face, like inefficient and expensive service delivery. The quality of health care can vary greatly, too.

Of course, it's not as simple as urban versus suburban versus rural. In reality, there is a continuum of options. There are suburban areas that have been molded to feel urban. There are suburban areas that feel so removed and bucolic that they resemble a rural environment.

There are rural areas that have a cluster of walkable amenities. Nonetheless, understanding what types of areas you prefer is important in determining your best set of options.

Managing trade-offs can be tricky. For example, if you want to live in the Southwest and in a suburban walkable area, few options exist. In Phoenix, there are only five such developments in the whole metropolitan area, including the urban core.[19] If walkability is important and there is flexibility in geography, then there are far more options in the Northeast, West, and to a lesser degree Southeast.

The move from the suburbs to the city for baby boomers has been written about extensively, but the media attention may be misleading. Most older adults live in the suburbs and have a preference to stay there.[20] With this in mind, one opportunity for planners and developers is to make suburban environments more attractive and suitable for people of all ages. Given the scale of the suburbs, this is not an easy task, but it is garnering increasing attention. Better, age-friendly living options in the suburbs may be around the corner.

NEXT STEPS AND ADDITIONAL
TOOLS AND RESOURCES

Choosing a place to live is a personal decision driven by emotion and logic. I know this firsthand. In our move from the Mid-Atlantic to Texas, we used what are known as high-level metrics—such as proximity of travel to other cities in the United States, projected growth and economic health, weather, and government policy—to narrow the field of metropolitan areas. An active lifestyle was important to us. We spent time talking to residents of Austin to get a feel for its ethos. We visited, met more people, and observed. In addition to driving, we walked, biked, and scootered to get a feel for different parts of the city and surrounding areas. Ultimately, we made a leap, but it seemed logical and emotionally felt right. It was a decision about finding and making a new home.

Moving away from a region, state, or metropolitan area can be difficult, particularly for people who have lived all or most of their lives there. This is what happened to my friend's father. In his 70s, he relocated from the Northeast to the Southwest to be closer to adult children and their families. It was a big change, more significant than anyone expected. He benefits from the peace of mind of having family close by should something happen. Even so, he has found it hard to make new friends and misses his close friends in the Northeast. A few years in, it is unclear whether moving was the right decision.

Most of us are not going to move to another region or metropolitan area, much less country. Understanding the trade-offs is important, however. Understanding the differences in areas can help spur action, even if a move is not involved. If your region is not making progress in becoming age-friendly, is there something you can do to promote change?

AARP's Livability Index offers an online analysis tool designed to inform policy, but it can also be helpful for individuals. Users input specific zip codes or addresses to understand and compare livability on a granular level. I find it helpful to compare both metropolitan areas and specific neighborhoods. The tool also allows for a change to the weight of variables so one can customize the analysis to individual priorities. For example, if living in a walkable neighborhood is important, you can set the dial to give it greater weight, and the overall score will change.

While regions, states, and metropolitan areas are significant and influence our lives, day-to-day lived experiences happen in neighborhoods, which is the focus of chapter 5.

CHAPTER 5

NEIGHBORHOOD AND COMMUNITIES

I'm a Mister Rogers groupie. I watched *Mister Rogers'*
Neighborhood as a young child, and I've seen numerous
movies about him as an adult. Fred Rogers's message of neighborliness, pertinent then, has become increasingly relevant today.

The trouble is that few of us know our neighbors. According to a
one study, only about one-quarter of people living in cities and suburbs profess to know all or most of their neighbors.[1] For older adults,
nearly half report knowing few or none of their neighbors.[2] Things
are trending in the wrong direction, too. According to another study,
about 20% of people regularly spend time with neighbors, down 33%
from the 1970s.[3]

A clear relationship exists between loneliness during midlife and beyond and connections with neighbors. Only 25% of those who know
most or all of their neighbors are lonely as compared to 64% of those
who know none of them.[4] Knowing neighbors improves well-being.
Researchers have found that people who feel connected to their neighbors have significantly fewer strokes than those who feel alienated.[5]

These connections matter not only at the individual level, but also
at the group level. These connections build social capital, or the networks of relationships among people who live and work in a particular

society, which enables that society to function effectively. Areas with social capital tend to operate better than those that don't.

Eric Klinenberg, a professor of sociology at New York University, studies the impact of social capital. In a groundbreaking study, he compared two demographically similar Chicago neighborhoods during a heat wave in the mid-1990s.[6] He found that more than six times as many people died in North Lawndale as in South Lawndale. He attributed the higher death rate to a difference in social connection. South Lawndale had a culture of stronger, more helpful relationships and had fewer residents living alone.

A fundamental question is whether our neighborhood and community bring out the best in us. If not, it may require relocation. More often, it involves an opportunity to better engage our existing community.

MIXED USE AND THIRD PLACES

Design matters. While Fred Rogers made a lasting impact on how we approach neighborliness, Jane Jacobs, a journalist and urban planning activist, left an imprint on how we think about carefully crafted neighborhoods. Her famous 1961 treatise, *The Death and Life of Great American Cities*, outlines her views on the conditions required to create a great neighborhood and elevate the lives of its residents. She was an early advocate for creating neighborhoods on a people scale and intermixing them with a variety of uses, such as retail, office, and residential. Today, we call this mixed use. She saw the benefits of intermingling uses and how it helped weave a community together, offering prescriptions around the number of residential units per block, length of a block, width of sidewalk, and more.

Jane Jacobs believed design could foster community by promoting social capital. Repeated social interactions with neighbors build familiarity and trust. As a result, the safety and well-being of the neighborhoods were looked after by the community more so than police and the health system. The health of the community is kept by an "intricate, almost unconscious network of voluntary controls and standards among the people themselves, enforced by the people themselves."[7]

While simply theories in Jane Jacob's era, the impact of design is now proven by research. High-amenity communities, ones with third places such as restaurants, bars, coffee shops, gyms or fitness centers, park or recreation centers, and community centers or libraries nearby, demonstrate increased trust, lower rates of loneliness, and a stronger sense of attachment to where we live.[8] People living in high-amenity areas are twice as likely to talk to their neighbors daily and are less likely to feel isolated from others, regardless of whether they live in large cities, suburbs, or towns. The mere presence of these amenities has a positive impact, irrespective of the frequency of usage. For older adults with amenities close by, the number of amenities and trip frequency did not make any difference in the level of perceived social connectedness.[9]

Grays Ferry Avenue Triangle is a triangle-shaped plaza in the Southwest Center City of Philadelphia that didn't exist a decade ago.[10] Previously, it was home to a handful of parking spots, a historic but inoperative water fountain, and a seldom used side street. Local residents, including a husband-wife team, came together and formulated a vision for the creation of a community gathering spot that would be closed to traffic and decorated with planters, painted asphalt, café tables, and a bike-sharing station. Today, the venue hosts an annual neighborhood festival sponsored by local businesses called Plazapaloolza, which includes live music, face painting, kids' carnival games, and food and drinks. Grays Ferry Avenue Triangle is an example of a successful third place that serves all ages.

NEIGHBORHOOD DESIGN AND THE 20-MINUTE NEIGHBORHOOD

Neighborhood design can have a key role in bringing people together beyond simply the existence of third places. The Congress for New Urbanism (CNU) is a leading voice around creating sustainable, human-scaled places where people can thrive. In effect, CNU takes the principles of Jane Jacobs's work and enhances them based on current ideas and issues. It advocates for the creation of neighborhoods that are compact, pedestrian-friendly, and mixed use, where daily pursuits can be accomplished within walking distance.

Seaside, Florida, in the state's panhandle, is perhaps the most significant development in New Urbanism, as it has inspired hundreds of similar developments coast to coast.[11] Built in the early 1980s, the community includes pedestrian- and bike-friendly streets, congenial gathering spots, and traditional architecture. It also incorporates a range of housing types at different price points, including small homes, apartments above retail shops, and backyard accessible dwelling units. Its purpose was to create a sense of community through design. It succeeded and was heralded as an "astounding design achievement" in *Time Magazine*'s "Best of the '80s Decade" issue. The development has aged well and remains a popular destination.

The 20-minute neighborhood, a derivative of the New Urbanism movement, is an emerging concept. It is anchored on the idea that most of what's needed for life should exist within a 20-minute public transportation trip, bike ride, or walk from home. These things include shopping, business services, education, community facilities, recreational and sporting resources, and jobs. It's all about helping people live locally. Melbourne, Australia, and Singapore feature the 20-minute neighborhood in their development plans. Two key ingredients to create these neighborhoods are sufficient development densities and a quality local public transportation service.

Enabling these new development approaches often involves changes to policy. Minneapolis has been a leader in this area in the United States. In 2019, after a prolonged process, the city changed its land policies to include more diverse housing options.[12] Previously, 70% of residential zoning only allowed single-family homes. To create a more diversified mix of housing options, the building code was changed to allow for "middle housing," like duplexes, triplexes, and quadplexes. Since this change, Oregon has altered its land-use policies, with other areas likely to follow.

Beyond neighborhood design, the orientation of the housing stock matters, too. Consider front porches. Front porches orient a house outwardly and offer an implicit invitation for engagement for those walking by. We experienced this firsthand in our neighborhood in Baltimore, where most homes had front porches. When the weather accommodated, we ate as many meals as we could outside. With our commotion and invitation to passersby, it was not uncommon for our dinner to spontaneously grow in size.

Indiana has taken the use of porches to another level.[13] Like Baltimore, Indianapolis has neighborhoods packed with homes with front porches. Joanna Taft, executive director of Harrison Center for the Arts, took advantage of this design element to spark social connection across the state of Indiana. For years, she observed a weekly ritual of neighbors visiting each other every Sunday afternoon in her neighborhood. She enjoyed the opportunities for social engagement, and it made a difference for all involved. Starting in 2014, she made a citywide event. Now it has become a statewide phenomenon, with the Indianapolis 500 as a sponsor and hundreds if not thousands participating.

Recognizing that most people need a gentle nudge, Taft's organization has created a guide and tools for people hosting porch parties. Their four steps involve: picking a day; inviting friends, family, and neighbors; preparing sharable food and drink; and creating easy ways to connect. Their guide includes specific suggestions for facilitating questions to help people connect. Examples include sharing neighborhood stories, participating in favorite traditions, and identifying ways to improve the neighborhood. And while porch parties occur in person, they use social media, including the hashtag #porchpartyindy, to help spread awareness and share successes.

Community design for most suburbs has shifted away from activating predominantly the front part of the house, such as porches, to the backyard. Likewise, front walks often connect to the garage and not to the public space. Such situations coupled with the prevalence of people driving cars make spontaneous interactions with neighbors less common. The standard course is to drive home into the garage, walk through the garage into the house, and cook and socialize in the backyard. It is not that the space can't be used for bringing people together, but it makes it more difficult for spontaneous interactions and is less welcoming. These design elements prioritize privacy over social connection.

These design preferences may be changing as a result of the coronavirus pandemic. Life in quarantine pushed people out to front yards for fresh air and the opportunity to intermix with neighbors at a safe distance. The lure of these positive interactions may create a draw to spend more time in the front of homes going forward. Landscape designers reported an increase in front outdoor spaces designed for social interaction as compared to before the pandemic.[14]

For other types of housing, like apartments and senior living, part of the neighborhood exists *within* the building. Common areas such as foyers, multipurpose spaces, and dining areas offer places to build community in planned and spontaneous ways. I have a senior living client in Seattle where most of the daily activity happens in and around the library. People stop by to read, socialize, and grab a cup of coffee—standard course in Seattle—and the library area is the venue of choice. No need for an invitation. Just show up.

While design can help make facilitate relationships and community, it's not necessarily enough. These spaces must be activated with life. There must be soul.

THE EVOLVING CULTURE OF NEIGHBORHOODS

A business school professor of mine once shared that every company has a distinct culture, whether they know it or not. Much is the same with neighborhoods. A neighborhood has a culture. It is invariably influenced by design, but it lives separate and apart from that. Culture evolves in potentially good and bad ways.

The neighborhood of Capitol Hill in southeast Washington, DC, is an interesting example. Not surprisingly, given its proximity to the nation's capital, the neighborhood's culture is one of intellectual curiosity and civic engagement. It is a neighborhood where parents are active in the local schools, volunteerism runs high, and neighbors care about each other. This history of engagement has followed the community as people have aged. This culture helped spawn Capitol Hill Village, an organization to help sustain and enrich the neighborhood's residents for the long term and part of the Village to Village Network.

While not the first, Capitol Hill Village (CHV) is one of the most successful villages in the country. CHV has more than 500 members, a viable business model, a strong intergenerational board, and a talented staff. It provides a wide range of services, including transportation, end-of-life planning, wellness activities, and social opportunities. Molly Singer, the former executive director, sees CHV as a "natural outgrowth of the catalytic neighborhood energies that started little leagues, a cooperative day school and the Capitol Hill Arts Workshop." The culture of the neighborhood is to get involved and look after each other, and this culture has fueled the success of CHV as a national example. As a result, Capitol Hill has a set of assets for older adults that don't show up in the physical design of the community.

Some neighborhoods are more conducive to successful aging than others. Part of the success of a neighborhood is its ability to attract the next generation. In so doing, it allows a range of resources, both monetary and social, to help support the full range of residents from babies to older adults. A number of these relationships are synergistic. Older residents can volunteer at local schools. Younger residents and families can help support older neighbors.

A strong neighborhood does not necessarily make it open to change, however. Most strong neighborhoods have tribe-like attributes. They are formed when people, in some way or another, are similar and band together for a common purpose. The problem is not necessarily with tribes, per se, but what happens when tribes become exclusive (when belonging is based on some form of superiority or breeds a protectionist mindset) and interested primarily in their own survival (when other tribes are viewed as a threat). In other words, difficulty arises when strong ties and likeness mutate into exclusion and conformity. When this extends to become an enclave, newcomers are unwelcome, and policies and design changes that attract younger people and families are not prioritized.

I witnessed this firsthand in our old neighborhood when protected bike lanes were introduced.[15] For decades, bike lane advocates in Baltimore have lobbied to expand bike infrastructure. Recent progress has been made, but not uniformly and not without incident. In our neighborhood, the addition of safe bike lanes was of value to young families but seen as an inconvenience to other residents. The process was not ideal—the city government asserted its right to create protected bike lanes without sufficient buy-in from the community. It led to intergenerational warfare almost literally. At a community meeting, older adults swore openly in front of kids, and at a later meeting, a fistfight broke out. Sadly, the conflict received national attention as an example of a dysfunctional neighborhood.

The true colors of a community can be revealed during certain events, like creating bike lanes. The key is to understand whether the culture of the neighborhood is open to others or closed off. If the community is closed off to change, like in our neighborhood, it will likely reduce the flow of younger people into the community and engagement in the neighborhood. This puts pressure not only on home prices—a key asset for older people—but limits the range of resources to help a neighborhood thrive.

A key question is whether your neighborhood—the existing one or one you'd like to be part of—is set up to be sustainably successful.

THE INTRA-NEIGHBORHOOD DYNAMIC

It's important to look at how a neighborhood interfaces with other neighborhoods in the area. Some neighborhoods behave more as enclaves, while others tend to have an influence that extends beyond their borders. Some neighborhoods can elevate others around them, in turn making additional neighborhoods and even the overall metropolitan area attractive to newcomers. On the flip side, when neighborhoods operate separately, there is a risk that the trajectory of a broader community is stuck in neutral or, worse, sliding backward, making it less attractive overall and for other neighborhoods as well.

When economic and racial segregation is high, neighborhoods with concentrated poverty or high levels of minorities tend to do disproportionately worse.[16] When neighborhoods are segregated, so too are schools, public services, jobs, and other kinds of opportunities that affect health. The effects of residential segregation are often stark: minorities who live in highly segregated and isolated neighborhoods have lower housing quality, higher concentrations of poverty, and less access to good jobs and education. They experience greater stress and have a higher risk of illness and death. Such segregation appears highest in the Northeast and Great Lakes region and is lowest along the southeastern seaboard.

Ultimately, there is a decision that neighborhoods need to make: Do we look out just for ourselves, or do we look out for our neighboring communities, too? The reality is that adjoining neighborhoods affect each other for better or worse. They can be seen as swimming in the same pool. You can't only clean the part of the pool you are swimming in.

This pool analogy comes from David Brooks and his book *The Second Mountain: The Quest for a Moral Life.*[17] Brooks is the founder of Weave: The Social Fabric Project, part of the Aspen Institute. Brooks and his colleagues are combing the country to find people, or weavers in their vernacular, that strive to make their community and neighborhoods more welcoming, joyful, and loving.

One example of a weaver is Leslie Fitzpatrick, a former health care executive in New Orleans.[18] Through a chance run-in with two preadolescent boys, she was shot in the face as part of gang initiation ritual. Once recovered, rather than distance herself from the broader community, she started APEX Community Advancement, an organization dedicated to helping gang kids in the greater New Orleans community. For the past decade, she and her husband have been dedicated to helping create a community for kids who don't have one through community centers, programming, and more. Leslie has worked beyond her immediate neighborhood to help those around her.

Simply put, some neighborhoods are stronger than others, and some are more oriented to reaching out to those beyond their borders. There is social capital that exists both within and beyond a neighborhood. It's important to understand what type of neighborhood is the best fit for you; whether you desire a neighborhood that is committed to supporting others, or one that is more isolated and exclusive.

NEIGHBORHOODS SHAPE US

As the real estate adage suggests, a home is all about location, location, location. On the surface, location can imply a desirable place based on proximity to desirable amenities, a quiet street, or a safe neighborhood. But the impact of a neighborhood can be much more profound, even down to the cellular level.

In her book *Friendship*, Lydia Denworth details some of the latest research on the dynamics of making friends and its impact on us.[19] Research has proven that friendship not only provides emotional support, but also influences our physical well-being and longevity. Your genes lay out the basic architecture of a human being—a menu of options for creating human proteins—but almost everything in terms of who we actually become, such as which proteins get made, is shaped predominantly by our environments. In other words, we're the joint product of a particular human genome and a particular life.

In this sense, our choice in a neighborhood influences our biological makeup. If our neighborhood brings out the best in us through meaningful friendships, physical activity, and so on, then we have optimized our genetics with an ideal set of environmental conditions. On the contrary, if a neighborhood breeds social isolation, loneliness, and a lifestyle that puts us at greater risk for chronic conditions, then we have likely not made the most of genetic predispositions.

Part of what's scary is the degree to which we are influenced by the people around us. We're even influenced by our friends' friends' friends. If our social network tends to be obese, we face a higher risk of obesity. If our social network is composed of happy people, we're more likely to be happy.

Therefore our choice in a neighborhood, in effect, is a choice to be part of a social network. We are likely to take on the characteristics of people from the neighborhood. If the prevailing culture is one of openness and hospitality, then we're likely to follow suit and host others. But if the attitude is more about privacy and people keeping to themselves, then we too are likely to be less welcoming to others.

A key question is whether the neighborhood is made up of people like you. There is robust research that shows how commonalities facilitate friendship. People are simply more likely to befriend others of the same gender, age, ethnicity, and so on. The pattern expresses itself all the way to the firing of neurons.[20] Taken too far, however, a community of people composed of people just like you could be also be stifling and boring. Perhaps a better question is whether a neighborhood is made up of *enough* people like you that you can spark friendships with.

Neighbors and broader community also provide a key element in starting and nourishing friendships: proximity. Researchers indicate that it takes about 50 hours to move from an acquaintance to a casual friendship, about 100 hours to call someone a friend, and over 200 hours of togetherness to become a best friend.[21] The challenge in our current era of busyness is that it is often hard to set aside time to get to know people. As we get older, we tend to not allocate enough time to nurturing friendships. In fact, in middle age, we allocate about 4% of our time for friends outside of family, and this number only increases to 8% for retirees.[22] In contrast, teenagers spend about 30% of their time connecting with friends outside of family.

Having close friends is critical regardless of location. Few of my closest friends have lived in my town. However, it is important to have a local network of friends who can be mutually supportive in a way that friends living in other geographies cannot. Beyond the practical reality of close support, spending time with friends in person allows for a level of connection that can't be replicated. For example, when two people look at each other, it triggers different neural activity than looking at a picture.[23] Further, direct eye contact with another person stimulates a call to action, a call to speak, and readiness for engagement. We need both lifelong friends that may live far away and a circle of friends in our immediate area.

As we age, people come in and out of our social circles. People move. Health changes. It requires attention to nourish existing friendships and create new ones. This requires effort and prioritizing friendship. Our neighborhoods also have an impact on our friendships. It is easier to make fast friends in some neighborhoods than in others.

UNDERSTANDING WHAT'S RIGHT FOR YOU

Finding the right neighborhood and community is an individual choice and comes with trade-offs. Some solutions are better than others. If you choose a neighborhood where the risk of social isolation and loneliness is high, this may affect your health and longevity. If you find a place that makes it difficult to be active, such as a neighborhood without sidewalks and surrounded by busy traffic, you are less likely to be physically fit, which may be detrimental to your health. If you feel out of place in your neighborhood, then finding good friends may be a challenge. It may never provide the comfort of home.

If you live in a neighborhood that you know and love, congratulations. Even better if it helps bring out the best in you through a strong social network and opportunities to stay active and engaged in life. In this situation, there is no reason to consider a change, save for other changes in your life such as shifts in health, finances, family, and mobility.

For most of us, there are elements of our neighborhood that we like and others we could do without. One of the keys is understanding which of these less desirable traits are controllable. If characteristics of the neighborhood that trouble you are out of your control—such as safety, lack of walkability, and lack of third places—and if these deficiencies trouble you, a change may be needed. But if the conditions that trouble you are controllable, such as not feeling a sense of community or having good friends close by, it may be a matter of taking initiative rather than making a change in location.

There are plenty of other ways to engage to make a neighborhood and one's experience in it better. There are ambitious examples, like Leslie Fitzpatrick's dedicated work in New Orleans. More commonly, however, steps one can take are small and incremental. It can be simply being more intentional about spending time with friends. Maybe it's going to a third place more often, like a coffee shop or park, and getting to know the regulars. Maybe it's volunteering at your local school. Such opportunities offer purpose, a strong personal connection to your community, and ways to meet new people. Maybe it's as simple as finding a group of friends to exercise with regularly. Maybe it's as simple as introducing, or reintroducing, yourself to your neighbors.

But what happens when the misgivings of the neighborhood are simply too great? This is when a physical change may be necessary. This is also when a move—the right move—can be beneficial.

Neighborhood matters a lot. It can affect you and your health in profound ways, down to the biological level. But just choosing a region, metropolitan environment, and a neighborhood is not sufficient. You need to determine the right physical dwelling for you.

PART III

WHAT IS THE RIGHT PLACE FOR YOU?

When most of us think of home, we think about a built environment. In this book, home is framed as more than a physical space. It comprises a broader region and metropolitan area. It is made up of a neighborhood, including third places. It is composed of personal networks. For many of us, home also evokes a powerful emotion. Home is a feeling.

Our built environment may be the most significant element of home. For many, home is a single-family house. But for those who live in cities, home may be an apartment, condominium, or co-op.

There is a wide range of options as we age. Sometimes, our thinking is limited to two disparate options: living in a single-family house or being cared for within a long-term care setting. This false binary choice misses the range of current and evolving options that can meet people's needs at a variety of life stages. Moreover, this thinking can naively expect too much of what's possible in a single-family house and unfairly undervalue senior living. There are circumstances for which living in a single-family house is ideal as we age, and others for which residing in senior living is a wise and satisfying choice. Conversely, conditions exist for which living in a single-family house can feel like a prison and an overwhelming burden, and in other situations, residing in senior living can be socially isolating and depressing.

It's important to understand the range of options, including the following types of housing:

- Traditional single-family houses and their siblings, such as townhomes, duplexes, triplexes, and quadplexes
- Apartments, including rental and condominium structures
- Age-restricted housing, such as 55+ houses and apartments
- Senior living, such as independent living, assisted living, skilled nursing, and life plan communities
- Emerging models, such as home sharing, cohousing, co-living, co-ops, and accessible dwelling units
- Family and intergenerational housing in various forms

The goal is to make any physical dwelling home. We will prefer some homes over others. By better understanding each option and its fit, we can assess which option is best for now.

This section looks at each of these options for built environments and provides a framework to evaluate them.

CHAPTER 6

SINGLE-FAMILY HOUSING

The single-family house and its siblings—townhomes, duplexes, triplexes, and quadplexes—represent the majority of housing inventory. For most older adults, living in a single-family house is the starting point. For some of these people, it is also the desired end point. Others would like to remain in a version of a single-family house but not the one they currently live in.

My friends James and Susan live in a single-family house they have owned since the 1970s. They have planned to stay in their home as they age. The coronavirus pandemic only heightened their interest in this approach. They are fortunate because they have a house where this is possible: open floor plan, low real estate taxes, and a strong social network, including family, in the area. They are also healthy and mobile.

Some older adults enjoy a single-family house but are drawn to a smaller space. Recall Mike and Lisa from chapter 2. In their move from Buffalo to Dallas, they decided to purchase a single-family house that is smaller and more manageable than their previous home. This approach enables them to commit less of their net worth to a house and keep ongoing costs lower. They chose to downsize but remain in a single-family house.

Others are attracted to variants of the single-family housing ilk, such as townhomes. This is the case for Krishna and Mamta. They move within Houston to be closer to friends and their Indian community. They decide to swap a single-family home for a two-story townhome. Its size is in line with their needs, and the location is within walking distance to stores and restaurants. It includes universal design features to facilitate aging, including an optional elevator.

There are also situations where staying in a single-family house may not be the wisest choice. There is a risk that while we may wish to stay in a single-family house, our health status doesn't fit well with the physical realities of the built environment. Suppose balance is an unacknowledged problem. The bathroom is fraught with fall risks: slippery tiles, bathtub to hurdle, or the absence of grab bars for extra support. Nearly one-third of older adults fall each year, events that lead to millions of emergency room visits and about 700,000 hospitalizations.[1] Just one fall, if severe enough, can dramatically change one's life trajectory. Under this scenario, no matter how much you love your current single-family home, it is not safe.

Teasing out the advantages and disadvantages will help sort out whether it is the right choice for you now.

ADVANTAGES

There are many advantages to living in a single-family house. First, ownership of a single-family house can provide a sense of independence and autonomy. Having our own space that we can design, modify, and decorate is central to the freedom to express ourselves. At the same time, it can serve as a refuge from the stresses of life.

Single-family homes tend to offer more space than other housing options. The typical single-family home has more than 2,500 square feet, which is almost twice the size of the average home the 1970s.[2] This additional space gives people room to be together and to be apart. Having a space in which one can be productive from home, of heightened interest during the COVID-19 pandemic, is important for many working people and even for retirees. Moreover, for older adults, a house can be large enough to host adult children and grandchildren or become settings for family gatherings. I have a several friends whose parents have kept their house or moved into another house to remain the base for extended family gatherings. Extra space can also come in the form of outdoor space, which can be a key asset in building social connections and communing with nature. Outdoor space can be a lifesaver in the context of a pandemic that requires physical distancing.

Single-family homeownership can be financially rewarding, having been a key wealth creator and a forced savings vehicle for millions of Americans. Home equity averages nearly $300,000 for the highest quartile of older homeowners.[3] While recent tax changes have made home ownership less attractive, owning a single-family home, particularly over a long duration, is likely a good investment, although there are other considerations when evaluating the financial attractiveness.

For many, living in a single-family home is the default option. A decision to live somewhere else has to overcome inertia. For couples, one partner may feel a need to change while the other may not. Not being on the same page typically leads to staying where you are. It's what's known. If it ain't broke, don't fix it, as they say.

But it can be more than that. The friction of moving, particularly for those who have lived in a house for decades, may be substantial. Reducing one's possessions may be an overwhelming task. The emotional and logistical costs of moving may seem to exceed the perceived benefits.

There are important differences between a single-family home and its siblings, like duplexes and townhomes. Duplexes, for example, offer an inherent trade-off of privacy and control for shared spaces and shared costs. Conversely, assuming you get along with the other residents in a duplex, it can be an opportunity for some natural, built-in social connection. Additionally, as these dwellings take up less space and tend to be in more dense developments, they are more likely to be located closer to amenities, like Krishna and Mamta's townhome is.

A good friend of mine, now in his 60s, has lived in a duplex for decades. At the time of his purchase, he could afford a duplex but not a single-family house in the neighborhood he desired. It worked well as he became close friends with his duplex neighbor. It is easy for them to look after each other's homes when the other is away. They also share some capital expenditures, such as for a new roof, and utility costs.

DISADVANTAGES

As we age, there are factors that make houses less attractive. For one, maintaining a house can become too much to manage. What was once joyful or tolerable becomes a burden. A friend in his 70s loves to spend time in his garden. It was a major hobby, bordering on an obsession. He had acres of flowers and vegetable gardens with a walking trail. The garden expanded to include koi ponds, statues, and a train set with remote controls. He loved spending time tending to it. But then, at one point, it simply became too much. It was not where he wanted to spend his time and energy. A desire for less outdoor space became a trigger to look for alternatives.

In other cases, we have too much indoor space. Rooms go unused. We overestimate how often family and friends visit. Perhaps houses of adult children become new hubs where people gather. The effort of cleaning and maintaining a house becomes too much and is not financially wise.

Maybe the physical design of the house is not desirable. The master bedroom is inconveniently on the second floor. The kitchen is not appealing and needs an expensive redesign. The house lacks the latest smart home technologies. Perhaps the house lacks universal design features that make living in it easier and safer. In such cases, the solution may be to remain in a house but downsize from the current one.

Single-family homes can also be socially isolating. Most single-family homes aren't in walkable, amenity-rich areas designed to bring people together, which can lead to more time spent alone. In a worst-case scenario for older adults, the four walls of a single-family house can feel like more of a prison that can be hard to escape to see other people. This is a particularly risky situation for people who can no longer drive.

For those that have lived in a house for a long time, the neighborhood around them has likely changed. In that process, as residents come and go, social networks change. What was once a life embedded in strong neighborly relationships can become devoid of community connections. In such a circumstance, despite a strong attachment to the house, the neighborhood may be a trigger for a change.

There are important financial considerations, too. Houses are generally more expensive to maintain than other options. Utility costs are higher as square footage increases. Annual real estate taxes can be substantial, in some cases topping 2% of the home's value. Regular repairs and maintenance are often more than most homeowners realize, and capital expenditures—such as carpet replacement, exterior painting, and roof replacement—can be expensive and difficult to predict.

Living in a single-family house often means you are on your own when needs arise. If care, whether for a long or brief period, is required, the responsibility falls on the individual to arrange services. In neighborhoods with single-family housing, because of the lack of density, these services tend to be more expensive than they would be in a congregate setting, such as apartments or senior living.

RENT VS. BUY

The common practice for single-family housing residents has been to own. Historically, renting a house has had limitations. Available rental stock is limited and often not high quality. Houses have tended to be managed by one-off owners. Getting appliances fixed, for example, can be a hassle. The net result is that it can be difficult to lease a house for the long term.

After the Great Recession of 2008, however, a shift began where single-family rental houses started to become more available and were increasingly professionally managed. This shift occurred as investment firms purchased housing stock with the plan to refurbish and rent properties as full-time rentals.[4] Renting a single-family home is now a viable option in many parts of the country. Real estate experts expect this trend to continue.

There are advantages to renting, particularly for older adults. First, the costs and effort for repairs, management, and capital expenditures remain the responsibility of the homeowner, not the renter. This makes housing-related costs more predictable and transparent, and it means maintenance is someone else's responsibility. Additionally, equity that would be tied up in a house can be used as part of a broader investment portfolio that can be customized to specific needs and risks. While housing has generally been a good investment, homeowners can have too much of their wealth allocated to real estate, representing lack of diversity and therefore a risk. The median older adult homeowner has about half of their net worth tied up in a home.[5]

Renters do not have a large portion of their net worth tied up in a house, thus providing for greater liquidity. For homeowners, if cash is needed and requisite assets are tied up in a home, it takes time to free up cash. The only options available are refinancing, assuming there is a capacity for additional leverage and financial markets are amenable, or liquidation of the house, but this too takes time and introduces risk. For example, during a recession, it may be difficult to sell a home at an attractive price or, in some cases, at all.

There are subtle but significant risks of homeownership. To sell your house, you need someone to buy your house. New generations bring different tastes and buying capacity. Some geographic markets grow, while others contract. An undesirable home in a contracting market presents challenges even during an economic period of broader growth. In particular, there is a growing concern that large homes owned by baby boomers may not be of sufficient interest to younger homebuyers.[6] This risk may be greatest in the Sunbelt.

Somewhat surprisingly, home values can be challenged in strong markets. One example is in the greater Washington, DC, market. Potomac, Maryland, is a beautiful suburb about 20 miles outside of downtown DC. The housing stock is almost exclusively single-family homes, often on large acreage, with little walkable access to amenities. With no metro access to DC and continued growth in the metropolitan area, gridlock traffic is increasingly common. As a result, while home values in the broader Washington, DC, market have almost universally increased, house values in Potomac have stayed flat or fallen.

At the same time, neighboring Bethesda, about 10 miles closer to DC, has seen significant growth and an increase in home values. Bethesda offers elements of what Potomac lacks: smaller lots, closer access to amenities, and viable metro access. Younger home buyers are eschewing large homes with large lots and a corresponding longer commute.

The calculus of whether renting or buying is the best option can be complicated. Homeowners need to consider the risks of being unable to sell a home either at a time frame or value desired. These considerations also need to factor the risk of health changes. Sometimes, life changes can necessitate immediate liquidity.

TECHNOLOGY IN THE HOME

Technology pervades all parts of our life, including single-family houses. The good news is that it is becoming easier for single-family homes to utilize technology to support our desires and needs. Working from home with phone, email, and video conferencing is becoming not only feasible, but also socially acceptable and in some cases a necessity. An increasing number of educational institutions are opening up their programs for long-distance learning, including curricula for lifelong learners. Health care systems are utilizing technologies like telehealth to help manage people's health without having to leave home.

Home security, for example, is rapidly changing with technology to make it better and more affordable. Do-it-yourself home security products provide streaming and recorded video through a wireless connection. Such technology enables residents to see who's at the front door at all times, even if they are not at home. With some options, you can speak to a visitor without coming to the door. Cameras and motion sensors can be easily installed throughout the house to alert homeowners of possible intruders. With smartphone access, people can manage the safety of their homes anywhere in the world.

Coupled with smart home technologies that enable remote locking and unlocking of doors, today's home security technologies have never been easier to deploy and manage.

These home technologies become even more powerful when they are used by multiple households within a neighborhood. People can share data or footage to help keep each other safe. With the increasing number of deliveries to homes, often when no one is around, thieves are taking advantage by stealing packages. With smart home security technologies, however, it is easier to alert neighbors to what is happening and help residents protect themselves. Video footage can also be used to help police track perpetrators.

There are some downsides to this technology, not the least of which of are security gaps and the possibility of hackers, but its continued advancement provides greater flexibility to live in a house of choice. These advances, in effect, may allow older adults to safely and conveniently live in their single-family homes longer than once anticipated.

HOME MODIFICATION

If an older adult wishes to stay in their existing single-family house, home modification can make that possible. Universal design is a design philosophy aimed at creating spaces that can appeal to a broad range of people, including those with mobility limitations.[7] Some of the principles apply broadly to the entire house, such as easy-lever door handles, no-threshold entries, and minimal use of stairs, particularly for heavily trafficked rooms; other modifications apply to specific rooms.

Modifications are most common in bathrooms and kitchens. For bathrooms, typical design elements include low- or no-threshold showers that minimize the effort to get in and out of the shower. Shower seats are also common, as are grab bars—or blocking to add grab bars in the future—and slip-resistant floor tiles and comfort-height toilets are popular as well. In the kitchen, it is about easy usability. Touch-controlled faucets can make it easy for people who have strength or hand control issues, as well as cooks with dirty hands to clean. Raised dishwashers and ovens can make it easier for those with more limited mobility or back issues. The design of shelving, including the use of pull-outs, can be made for easy access.

There are several other areas to consider, too. The location of the master bedroom can be significant. For multiple-story homes, if the master bedroom is on the second floor, it can be enough of an inconvenience to prompt a move. At a minimum, having a first-floor bedroom that could be converted to a master bedroom adds flexibility. It is also important to consider furniture and furniture layouts. Rugs can be unintended trip hazards. Poor lighting and awkward furniture positioning can increase the risks of falls. Remodels may want to consider an area where caregivers and family could stay for a prolonged period of time.

One misconception is that utilizing universal design principles makes a home feel institutional and medical. In most cases, principles of good design can be worked seamlessly into fashionable homes. It often just requires careful planning on the front end of a renovation. The incorporation of universal design principles can also make it easier for visiting families with young children.

If one's plan is to stay in a single-family house, it is unlikely that a single home modification will address all of one's needs over time. Instead, changes and tweaks are constant as needs shift and new options emerge.

EVOLVING OPTIONS

For those interested in single-family homes, options other than staying in an existing house continue to grow. Real estate developers are recognizing the housing demand from baby boomers looking to downsize and live closer to amenities. One such developer is EYA, an innovative homebuilder that focuses on housing in urban neighborhoods. Since 1992, the company has built more than 5,000 homes in more than 40 neighborhoods across the Washington, DC, metropolitan area and has twice been named America's Best Builder by Builder

Magazine. EYA has focused increasingly on building quality townhomes in walkable areas.

EYA's projects include a number of design elements that resonate with older adults. Their townhomes generally range from 2,000 square feet to 3,500 square feet—spacious but not overwhelming. Elevators are optional. Townhomes include modern kitchens and outdoor spaces for entertaining. They are attractive and include elements of universal design, such as minimal-threshold showers with seating. They also offer integration of smart home technologies and space for a home office.

Large homebuilders are improving product designs to appeal to the aging consumer market. Many are incorporating elements of universal design, particularly in the bathrooms and kitchens, as well as offering customization to make a new home more suitable for older adults. Lennar, one of the nation's largest homebuilders, offers a model that creates space for multigenerational living, considering what's needed both in design and spacing.

Policymakers have begun to increase housing density to minimize sprawl and improve housing affordability. With cities like Minneapolis modifying zoning to include duplexes, triplexes, and quadplexes in addition to single-family housing, real estate developers have an opportunity to develop more housing for a range of consumers, including older adults. The advantage of this housing is similar to EYA's model: these housing units are closer to amenities than traditional suburban new developments.

Innovative models are making it easier for people at a range of wealth levels to live in existing housing as they age. Sarah Szanton, a professor and researcher at Johns Hopkins University School of Nursing, co-developed CAPABLE, or Community Aging in Place—Advancing Better Lives for Elders, a successful, nationally recognized program that operates in 17 states.[8] The program integrates a registered nurse, an occupational therapist, and a licensed handyman to work with older adults to support them where they live, usually in single-family homes. CAPABLE typically works with low-income urban dwellers and is funded based on savings in the health care system, such as fewer days in institutional long-term care settings. CAPABLE should be a national model for people of all incomes.

BEST PRACTICES AND NEXT STEPS

Single-family house living has a lot of benefits, notably independence and autonomy. An important question is whether it meets your current desires and needs. The answer can be "yes" as a type of living environment but "no" for your current single-family house. Your current house may be too large, too expensive, or unsafe. Keep in mind the option to live in a single-family house, just not your current one.

If you live in a single-family house, assess the costs and benefits based on today's reality. Be sure to list all of the costs, including the opportunity costs of equity in your home, if applicable. Mapping your desires and needs as well as the costs and benefits may help crystallize the appropriateness of your current house.

One thing to consider is whether a single-family house or one of its siblings, such as a townhome, duplex, triplex, or quadplex, is the better option. Particularly with zoning rights easing in some municipalities, a new supply of townhomes and duplexes may offer age-friendly designs that provide the benefits of single-family housing with some other benefits to boot. It is worth researching what's available. This turned out to be the best option for Krishna and Mamta.

For adult children, a similar exercise of outlining desires and needs, costs and benefits as you see them for your loved one may be valuable. You could facilitate a conversation with your loved one to understand where there are gaps in perspectives. Particularly if a house will be key in funding care in the future for a loved one, you may want to understand the value of the house and market dynamics. In some instances, if there is a concern about the viability of selling a house in the future, getting prepared for a sale with the help of a broker may be wise. Selling too early is much better than not being able to sell later if funds are needed to support a loved one.

CONCLUSION

Tens of millions of Americans prefer and can afford to live in single-family housing. With planning, this product can work well as we age. Doing so will likely involve modifications in the physical space and our behaviors, however. In essence, our desire for control and independence makes a single-family home more attractive while simultaneously putting a greater burden on the individual to manage life, which can be increasingly complex as one ages. Other dwelling options, such as apartments, handle this trade-off differently.

CHAPTER 7

APARTMENTS

Several years ago, I had an idea. What if apartments could be better designed and operated to cater to the well-being of people of all ages? Since successful aging is more about lifestyle than DNA, what if apartments could help nudge residents into healthier lifestyles, such as one with a greater sense of purpose, social connection, and physical activity?

This idea led to a partnership with a national real estate developer to create The Stories at Congressional Plaza in Rockville, Maryland, a suburb outside of Washington, DC. The Stories brand speaks to the fact that each of us is writing our story, and in the age of longevity, we have the opportunity to live out additional chapters. Why not make these additional chapters as rewarding and meaningful as possible?

The Stories consists of approximately 200 apartment units in a walkable, mixed-use location with nearby amenities such as a grocery store, coffee shops, retail shops, and a Metro station. The building was designed with all ages in mind. Living units have universal design features, including bathrooms with showers and benches, slip-resistant tiles, and blocking to add grab bars, as well as kitchens with roll-out shelving. Residents can customize living units with paint, accessories, and technology add-ons. Units are rentals, with multiple lease terms up to three years.

The operating model is designed around three principles: connection, access, and simplicity. With connection, efforts are made to help people get to know each other, through regular community-driven events and resident-led get-togethers, like potlucks and game nights. With access, relationships are forged with third-party services providers, from dry cleaners to fitness coaches to health providers. In regards to simplicity, the essence of the experience is to make life easier so that residents can focus on what is most important to them. The operating model hinges on the role of a lifestyle ambassador, which serves as part concierge, part life coach, and part service coordinator.

The model at The Stories worked. People across multiple generations moved in, including millennials, Gen Xers, baby boomers, and even some from the Greatest Generation. Residents appreciated the thoughtful approach. Friendships formed, including intergenerational ones. Newspaper articles and magazines wrote about the project, and I spoke at national conferences, including a TED-like talk on the concept.[1]

While The Stories has unique features that make it particularly suitable for older adults, apartments in general are an appealing option for many people. About 40 million people live in apartments, including about 10 million people 65 and older.[2] It's a rapidly growing product type, particularly in urban and dense suburban environments. A key driver is attainability: apartments are typically more affordable than single-family homes. An increasing number of people, including older adults, are choosing this type of living environment. Industry experts call this cohort "renters by choice." Indeed, today's apartments are different than they were for past generations.

Think back to Robert and Lucinda. They moved from New Jersey to Seattle to be close to family. They also choose to live in an apartment in the city. Downsizing and living in small quarters posed some initial challenges, but they benefited from easy access to amenities of urban living and social connection to their neighbors in their apartment building.

Like houses, apartments can be rented or owned. Most buildings tend to be one or the other, and there are trade-offs with each option.

ADVANTAGES

One motivation to live in an apartment is simply to downsize, or "right-size" as some say, and simplify life. Reduce the amount of stuff. Spend less time on home maintenance. Focus time and energy on what's most important to you. Enable more of a lock-and-leave lifestyle, where it is easy to pick up and go when you want. Many of today's apartments are managed by professional companies that excel at handling service requests down to changing light bulbs. There is a peace of mind that a streamlined lifestyle can provide.

There is a trade-off of less private space for more shared space elsewhere in the apartment building and neighboring areas. There is little need for a home gym with a gym in the building. It can be less important to have a home office if there is space for working in the building or at a nearby coffee shop. Catering kitchens can be places to cook communally with friends. Shared outside spaces can supplement a small private balcony.

For those who wish to be in walkable areas near amenities, single-family housing typically is often not an option because of density. Policymakers focus on greater population densities around amenities such as grocery stores and retail and may not permit single-family housing. For those who value walkability, apartments may be the best path to achieve such a lifestyle.

Another advantage is proximity to others. It is harder to be physically or socially isolated when others live nearby and there are opportunities for interaction. In effect, each apartment building is its own neighborhood, with opportunities for people to get to know each other. Unlike some other more communal communities like cohousing, living in an apartment building offers an invitation to engage in the community, but it is not a requirement. It can be a good balance that works for both the introverted and extroverted.

Apartments provide opportunities for intergenerational engagement. The Stories has fostered a number of intergenerational relationships, including one between a retired school teacher, Judy, and Katherine, a homeschooled teenager. Judy volunteered to tutor Katherine, improving her French and sparking a friendship. They spent time with each other doing other things, including sharing meals, knitting, and playing games. A valuable intergenerational relationship was made possible by proximity and a culture that brought people together.

Apartments tend to create and invigorate third places. Some of these third places may exist within the residential building. It could be around a coffee station in the foyer, in a reading area by the fireplace, or in a game room. Pools can be a key spot during warm months. It can also happen in the neighborhood outside. If an apartment building is close to traditional third places, such as a coffee shop, library, or community center, residents benefit from easy access and opportunities to connect with others outside the apartment community.

Access to services can be easier and less expensive when there is a high density of people. For delivery services, like dry cleaning, it is less expensive for a service provider to make one stop to reach many people than to make individual stops. In other words, some services can be provided to an apartment building that can't be profitably or efficiently offered to single-family houses. This can be especially true for health care service providers. Health care services, such as home care, can provide lower costs and greater availability to those living near others that need similar services.

Apartment designs and operations have adapted to our changing lifestyles. Nearly half of apartment dwellers are single.[3] For many people, especially those living alone, having a pet is increasingly common and provides companionship. Fortunately, living with a pet in an apartment has never been easier. An increasing number of apartments allow pets, and some high-end apartments include dedicated common spaces for pets—even dog-washing stations. Apartment communities are recognizing that pets are part of the family and need to be treated as such.

Housing budgets are an important consideration for many. Especially for older adults who rely more on a fixed income, rental apartments offer predictable housing costs, particularly over the leasing term. Some locales even have limits on rent increases for older adults, providing greater financial predictability. There are no unexpected capital expenditures, like the replacement of a roof or furnace, that become the responsibility of the renter. There are simply fewer surprise housing costs. For older adults, certainty in expenses is particularly valuable.

The financial flexibility that apartments offer is a key benefit. If preferences or life circumstances change, it is easier to switch to a different housing option at the end of a lease. Even a change needed before the end of a lease is possible, as landlords will typically work with you. As we age, the conditions for which a change may be desirable can be numerous, ranging from health considerations to lifestyle preferences to circumstances with extended family. This option of financial flexibility has real value.

Perhaps most importantly, apartment living is typically less expensive than similar single-family housing options. House value appreciation can be a critical factor—markets with high home appreciation strengthen the argument for owning a house—but otherwise the costs of renting are favorable. For one, living within a larger building, particularly with less space, tends to result in lower utility costs. In addition, real estate taxes can be quite high for single-family owners; for renters, these costs are embedded in rent and tend to be lower.

An often-overlooked element of comparing the cost of owning versus renting is the opportunity cost of equity in an owned house. For example, some homeowners who own their house outright, not uncommon for older adults, see a rental apartment as more expensive than living in their current house. With no mortgage costs, their monthly outflow is based on utility costs, real estate taxes, repairs, and capital improvements. The challenge with this thinking is that it misses the return on alternative investments versus a house.

Let's use an example. If a 100% owned home is worth $500,000 and is subject to a modest appreciation of 2% per year, the annual return on investment of equity in the home is $10,000, or $833 per month. If instead this capital was invested in the stock market and returned 7% per year, it would yield $35,000 per year, or $4,167 per month. This difference, $25,000 on an annual basis or $2,083 every month, is sizeable. Leverage on a home can change some of these economics but also changes the risk profile. Regardless, an analysis must focus on value, not just monthly cash flows when comparing a rental apartment versus an owned single-family home.

For apartment condominiums, there are some other advantages to consider over rental apartments. One, people tend to stay longer. It is easier to make and continue friendships in a living environment when people make it more their home and stay awhile, as transience makes community building more difficult. In addition, home modification is easier in a condominium. While condos have homeowner associations (HOAs) that set parameters for changes, it is typically easier to change a physical environment when you own it. To a more limited extent, changes can be done with apartments, but capital improvements are typically retained by landlords, who may require a security deposit that ensures the apartment is returned to its original condition.

DISADVANTAGES

One of the principal disadvantages to apartment living is having limited personal space inside and outside. For those used to living in a suburban single-family house, an apartment can feel small and confining. For older adults accustomed to having their own space, apartment living can take some time to get used to. Plus, particularly for rental apartments, making significant changes, like moving walls to change room configurations, is not possible. For green thumbs used to creating their own outside spaces, apartments offer limited options. Sometimes there are community gardens and other outdoor spaces that residents can use, but it's not the same as having your own garden. It can be a challenge for some people to make an apartment feel like home.

This lack of space is felt more intensely during a pandemic like COVID-19. Quarantining in a small space can be challenging and even depressing. It can be made worse if there are not accessible outdoor spaces to effectively create more usable space. The impact of small spaces during the time of an international health crisis is no longer a theoretical exercise. It must be considered and may tilt things toward the flexibility of a rental apartment versus a condominium apartment.

One of the advantages of apartment living can also be a challenge: other people. Apartments can be loud. Many people living in close proximity leads to sound reverberating throughout the built environment. There tends to be noise in general and at all hours, and for those not living on the top floor, sounds can come from above.

There is also a risk that other people in the apartment building are not part of your tribe. You may have little in common or find it hard to connect. And for that reason, despite being around others, apartment living can be lonely. Recall that loneliness is subjective; people can be around others and feel lonely. The feeling of being disconnected yet among others can be particularly challenging for people living large apartment complexes and buildings that do little to cultivate a sense of community among residents. Sadly, there are too many apartment buildings and not enough apartment *communities*.

My friend Gabriel experienced a lack of community when he moved to an urban rental apartment building. A divorcee in his 60s, he relocated from the suburbs and loved the short commute and access to the downtown amenities. Looking for new friends, he participated in social events hosted by the apartment, often with people who were much younger. He enjoyed the vibe and opportunity to meet people different than him, but he didn't meaningfully connect with anyone.

After several years, the novelty of downtown living wore off, and he moved to the suburbs to be closer to family and friends. It was a fun but short chapter, and probably not a living situation he will try again.

In most apartments, as in single-family homes, you are on your own. If health care needs arise, the responsibility falls on the individual to figure them out. For technology, the individual must determine, purchase, and configure systems—they can't rely on apartment staff to help. For older adults and their families, it is important to understand the limitations of apartment living. You can't assume that because you live among others that there is built-in infrastructure or an obligation for others to help when support is needed.

Rental apartments have some additional disadvantages. Resident turnover is high in most buildings. The average tenure of a resident is approximately two years.[4] Put another way, a building loses half of its residents each year on average. Some buildings experience lower resident turnover. They tend to be where residents consider their apartment their home and have invested in making it feel that way. Resident turnover matters because it is hard to make lasting friendships if neighbors are transient. It can also create a short-term mindset that makes people less willing to invest in relationships if there is an expectation that residents won't be there long.

Rent increases can be a challenge, too, particularly for people dependent on a fixed income. Rent increases are core to apartment living. The industry employs daily pricing to account for fluctuations in supply and demand. As a result, apartment buildings are more likely to increase rent in markets where high demand is high. High-demand markets tend to be places where people want to live. This is part of the quandary. Some markets have rent control or measures in place to limit rent increases for older adults. Another mitigation measure is to sign a longer lease term, where rent increases are agreed upon in advance and may be smaller.

There is one key financial downside of rental apartments: there is no ownership interest. Renters are neither able to take advantage of federal and state tax deductions nor share in the upside of real estate appreciation. Deciding to rent versus own is a matter of weighing the risk and reward; you may determine that the financial risks of home-ownership may outweigh the rewards.

Another risk is apartment management and ownership changes. Because apartments are a popular investment vehicle, apartments are regularly bought and sold. As a result of ownership changes and for other reasons, management companies change, too. These changes can negatively affect resident experience. For one, it can lead to increased employee turnover. It can also lead to changes in policy, such as how maintenance requests are handled or a hike in rental rates. Potential changes in management and ownership in particular can make the long-term resident experience unpredictable. A great living situation risks becoming less so. This risk can be mitigated by moving into buildings owned by long-term owners, such as real estate investment trusts (REITs) or private owners with long holding periods.

Condominium apartments have a separate list of disadvantages. HOAs are notorious for being problematic. First, HOAs typically include monthly fees to run and maintain the building. These fees can be substantial. Also, boards of HOAs can be political, producing factions focused on competing priorities. For example, one constituency may be interested in minimizing monthly fee increases, while another may be focused on discretionary capital improvement projects, like remodeling an entryway. These tensions can affect the tenor of the community. Further, if the building is not managed or maintained well, it can be difficult to sell existing units. In some cases, HOAs can make it difficult to facilitate aging in your unit. Certain technology changes may not be permitted in the building, or there may be resistance to substantial physical changes in your unit.

I experienced the challenges of HOAs firsthand as a consultant to an urban condominium apartment building. I was contacted by the management company to help older residents understand how best to design their living situation for successful aging. A number of the required changes, including updating technology access to the building, were blocked by the HOA. Several older residents were forced to sell their unit and move out because necessary accommodations were not approved.

What is clear is that if control and privacy are important to you, apartments have significant downsides. Some of these downsides can be mitigated, but not fully.

EVOLVING OPTIONS

The number of apartments has grown substantially over the last several decades, and so, too, have the types of apartments and price points. Part of what has changed is the quality of the apartments. Particularly among high-end apartments, standard features include a contemporary open floor plan, granite countertops in the kitchen, modern appliances, an in-unit washer and dryer, spacious closets, and more. They have attractive and spacious amenities, ranging from state-of-the-art fitness centers, demonstration kitchens, swimming pools, coworking spaces, and more. These communities also generally make accommodations for pets.

Apartment owners understand how important it is for them to have residents stay after their initial lease term. An increasing number of managers are enhancing the breadth of their services and facilitating social connections among residents. More buildings have concierges that help with building logistics, package delivery, and coordination of simple services, like dry cleaning. These communities host regular social events within and near the apartment building.

On top of these trends, apartment owners recognize that older adults, baby boomers in particular, are a large and growing demographic, and the ability to appeal to them is good for their business. Therefore, for some communities, amenity spaces and programming are customized in some fashion to appeal to older audiences or is at least mindful of incorporating residents of all ages.

Apartment living options for older adults are growing both in urban and suburban locations. What may not have existed five years ago may be available in your market. And what may not exist today may be available soon. Innovations in building design, construction, and technology have the prospect of offering greater value to older consumers in the future.

BEST PRACTICES AND NEXT STEPS

If apartment living is appealing, finding the right place is key. Get a sense of where you'd like to live in terms of location and size of apartment building. There is often a trade-off with size. Small buildings provide the intimacy to get to know other residents but offer few amenity options. Large buildings can be overwhelming with the sheer number of residents but often provide a wide range of amenity options. A word of caution on size: if a community is small, fewer than 100 units, there may not be a large number of older adults to connect with within your building.

While location and size are easy to research, other important elements require more work. For one, it is important to get a feel for the type of people living in a community. Communities are not legally allowed to share the demographics of a community, such as age, ethnicity, or education level. But you can learn some of this information by talking to people. When meeting with a leasing agent, it is important to share your needs and desires. Ask for examples of current residents that fit a similar profile. You can also ask for a list of community events and see if it's possible to attend one. Ask if you can speak to a resident ambassador. If such a person doesn't exist, the culture may not be oriented toward the community. Furthermore, some buildings have guest rooms or rooms that tenants sublease. There could be an option to try out a community before making a commitment.

Some communities, more often condominiums than rental apartments, function unofficially as naturally occurring retirement communities, or NORCs. These communities tend to attract a disproportionate number of older adults who consider their apartment to be home for the long term. People may live in NORCs for many years or even decades. As a result, they tend to have a stronger, resident-driven culture where people know each other and socialize regularly. NORCs don't officially list themselves as such, but word of mouth can help you find one.

Researching the management company and owner is an important step. You can find some of this information when speaking to a leasing agent; Internet research can help you learn more. Be sure to look at online reviews of the community and the management companies. Be wary of investment firms with short-term investment horizons as owners. They tend to sell properties more frequently, and each sale introduces risks, including a change in the management company. Long-term holders, like REITs, tend to own their real estate assets for many years, often decades, and are incented to invest in and manage their communities for the long haul.

Push landlords on leasing terms. Leasing agents and community managers are incented to maintain a high occupancy. Older adult tenants can be attractive to apartment owners, as they generally move less often and are more likely to pay rent on time. Don't be afraid to negotiate on terms that matter to you, such as the length of lease, visibility on rent increases, ability to customize or modify your living space, and more.

If you are already in an apartment and have concerns about whether it is the right place for you in the future, set up a meeting with the building manager and outline things that are important to you. The manager's receptiveness and degree of influence within the organization will help you determine whether a change is in the offing should your needs change.

CONCLUSION

Rental apartments and to lesser degree condominium apartments offer less control than owning a single-family house. But they have a long and a growing list of benefits. Apartments suitable for older adults are increasing in availability and popularity. Apartment living often offers proximity to people of all ages, which can lead to forging intergenerational relationships. Particularly in locations where age-friendly initiatives have taken hold, one should expect more apartment buildings that are designed for all ages and conducive to successful aging, like The Stories at Congressional Plaza.

For a subset of older adults, however, living around people just like them, at least as defined by age, is most desirable.

CHAPTER 8

AGE-RESTRICTED HOUSING

The Villages is mind blowing. An age-restricted master planned mecca in central Florida that encompasses more than 30 square miles, The Villages boasts a population of more than 100,000 residents. It was the fastest-growing metropolitan area in the United States between 2010 and 2017, growing more than 30%. Growth continues with no end in sight. Following seven straight years as the top-selling master planned community in the country, The Villages is arguably the most successful such community in the United States.

It offers a wide range of amenities, activities, and housing options. As its name suggests, The Villages is organized in a series of villages. Each of its thirteen villages is composed of housing, recreation centers, and commercial centers, often in the form of walkable town centers. Golf is featured prominently, and virtually every recreational activity is available, including but not limited to swimming, bocce, shuffleboard, tennis, pickleball, and yoga. It hosts its own Senior Games, where approximately 2,000 people compete in hundreds of athletic events. Parks, dog parks, and fitness trails are scattered throughout. The Villages has nearly 3,000 resident-led clubs. Its entertainment venues have attracted topflight talent, including Willie Nelson, the Beach Boys, Jerry Lewis, and other music legends. It boasts a television station, radio station, and a daily paper with a circulation in excess of 40,000 subscribers.

The Villages is a national and international draw. When I visited, a board in the sales center detailed names and locations of new residents or "newest villagers" moving in over several days. It included 69 family units from 23 states ranging from Hawaii to Maine, and one from Canada. About two-thirds of the people were moving from outside of Florida. The makeup of residents leans older, of course; as of 2018, the median age for the Villages was 67.4, almost 30 years older than a typical American. It is generally a well-educated lot with the health and financial resources to enjoy their retirement.

The sales agent characterized the draw for people to move considerable distances in one word: lifestyle. The lifestyle of social engagement, physical activity, intellectual engagement, and entertainment is compelling.

While The Villages may be an outlier in its success and scale, age-restricted housing is not a new phenomenon. For-sale age-restricted communities are commonly referred to as active adult communities. The concept was pioneered in the 1960s by Del Webb with his iconic Sun City master planned community in Arizona, which drew national attention and a cover story in *Time Magazine*. Today, active adult communities scatter the country, from typical retirement destinations in Arizona and Florida to smaller communities outside of suburban areas. They all follow a similar formula: attractive and attainably priced homes, desirable amenity spaces, and an active social schedule.

Niche active adult communities have entered the market as a way for prospective residents to find their kin. None has garnered more national attention than Margaritaville, where retirement living meets Jimmy Buffett fans, or Parrot Heads as they are known, in paradise. Daily live music and extended happy hours feature prominently. But Margaritaville has a broader appeal. It resonates with people who want fun and carefree living to be central in their lives. This commonly shared value helps create a sense of community among residents. Margaritaville has three communities, with plans for more.

A suburban rental apartment version of active adult communities has also entered the market. Leveraging successful practices for apartment living and incorporating amenities and social engagement activities from for-sale active adult communities, these age-restricted rental communities offer the active adult lifestyle but at a smaller scale and with closer proximity to major metro markets. These apartments allow older adults to live with their peers while also being close to friends and extended family that may live in the broader area. These apartments are typically priced at a premium as compared to conventional apartments owing to the higher costs to build and operate them.

ADVANTAGES

The biggest advantage of active adult communities is that they offer an onramp for social engagement with peers. It can feel like college, only decades later. Knowing that everyone is in a similar life stage with spare time can make it easier for making personal connections and developing relationships. A friendly culture, something that The Villages cultivates and markets, makes it easier for new residents to integrate into the community. Particularly for solo agers, having a built-in social life can be attractive. This dynamic stands in contrast to living alone in an oversized single-family home in the suburbs. It can be a remedy for loneliness and social isolation.

When communities are large or affinity based, the odds of finding your tribe increase. Most of these communities depend on resident-led social engagement, like clubs for knitting, poker, and so on. These clubs require leaders and active participants, creating opportunities for residents to get to know each other.

Think back to Mike and Lisa and their move from Buffalo to Dallas. They decided to live in a single-family house in an age-restricted community. It enabled them to downsize and connect with a peer group in a new city. This decision eased their transition.

There are design advantages as well. When developers have a narrow target market, they are able to design living and communal spaces that best cater to this market. Housing design in active adult communities attractively incorporates universal design principles. Developers can create floorplans specifically designed for visiting grandkids or remote working. Amenity spaces are optimized for social engagement and popular uses. For example, pickleball courts, a rare amenity in other communities and popular with older adults, are commonly incorporated in active adult communities. Not only do active adult communities offer amenity spaces that resonate with older adults, they often dedicate more space than comparable non-age-restricted communities.

Active adult communities' staff create regular customized programming for residents. Social calendars are packed with activities, often offering more than one could possibly do. It leads to the refrain that retirees in these communities are busier than ever before.

These communities are disproportionately located in places that are attractive for older adults. They are overrepresented in the Southeast and Southwest, states with warm and sunny weather. Further, a number of these locations are in tax-friendly states such as Arizona, Florida, and Texas. For people looking for a wholesale plan for retirement living, active adult communities located in a senior-friendly state can represent an attractive package.

Although living in an age-restricted setting can seem insular, most communities offer opportunities to engage in the broader community. Active adult developments in suburban areas or rental active adult buildings located in walkable areas are not far from the mainstream world. Residents may be proximate to local coffee shops, libraries, and community centers, enabling them to engage with the broader, intergenerational society. Volunteer clubs create opportunities for regular civic engagement, and for larger communities there are events like craft fairs and speakers that attract people from outside to visit the community. Plus, with technology, there are increasing ways to engage with people virtually.

Financial considerations are similar to the factors for single-family ownership and rental apartments.

DISADVANTAGES

Moving into an active adult community, particularly when an interstate move is involved, is risky. It can be a big change to move from a single-family home in a suburban neighborhood to a master planned community composed of older adults. You may think you'll love it, but you may not. If you don't, it is difficult and costly to unwind your decision and re-create your old life.

One of the biggest critiques is that it seems unnatural. To be in place where younger people are excluded can feel like an alternative universe. An active adult community may feel initially like a fun and exciting fantasy land, but it lacks the richness and depth of intergenerational interactions. Some critics call it an example of "age apartheid" and see it as perpetuating the age segregation that is already pervasive in our culture.

I experienced this firsthand at the sales center for Margaritaville as I inquired for an older family member. The sales associate was quick to point out features like spacious homes, swimming pools, fitness rooms, and live music venues. The fact that kids weren't allowed was pitched as a key feature. In fact, the agent was careful to emphasize, "We've designed this so it's as if kids don't even exist. Isn't that great?" For some that may be great, but for others, it may dissuade them from taking the next step.

Others are turned off by active adult communities because they can feel too insular. There is an attraction to knowing that there are people of a similar life stage that can make it easier for connection, but there can be a blandness when everyone seems the same. In other words, the lack of diversity in age can carry over to a lack of diversity in other areas, too, including political views, life experiences, and interests. For those who are concerned about sameness, it can be a challenge to escape.

Some of the strongest critics claim that active adult communities cheat residents of the richness of life. Purpose based on fun has limitations. Purpose that is focused on deeper meaning has been linked to stronger health outcomes. Put simply, what happens when the fun turns into boredom?

A breaking point can occur suddenly. This was the case with my friend Bill. He lived in an age-restricted community for about 10 years. He was active socially and a member of the resident's association. One day, however, it struck him that he wanted to be in a normal neighborhood with people of all ages. Being around only older people had grown tiresome for him. He sold his house—using some of the proceeds to buy a sports car—and moved into a single-family house in a conventional neighborhood. He stayed in touch with his friends from his prior community, but it was the right change for him.

There's another risk: What happens when the party ends? Typically, the first wave of residents is younger older adults actively engaged in the community and programming. At some point, however, as natural aging occurs, residents aren't as involved in the activities because of either waning interest or health limitations. This can change the feel of the community. It may still be valuable for residents, but it is different. Residents need to be prepared for this change. It may not necessarily feel like the paradise they originally moved into.

Along the same lines, these communities typically neither provide health care service nor coordinate services from third-party providers. Much like single-family homes and apartments, residents are left to their own devices to manage health care needs as they arise. For large communities, like The Villages, some health centers or senior housing providers are co-located or adjacent to the development.

For-sale active adult communities also represent financial risk. For some communities, the demand for housing can be greatest on the initial sellout and then dissipate over time. As residents and the community age, demand may wane. The value proposition may not resonate with the next generation of older adults. When this happens, it can be problematic for homeowners needing to sell to access funds for other needs, such as for care. One should not assume that age-restricted homes trade at the same pricing level and speed of conventional houses in the area.

Rental active adult communities include a different set of risks. Just like for normal rental apartments, residents need to look out for outsized rental increases. But the bigger risk is that the community changes in a more fundamental way. Some active adult communities are designed to be converted into senior living, with meals and care provided. This conversion is typically a right of the building owner and does not require renter consent. The net result is that terms can change, requiring certain services, like daily meal service, as part of the rental agreement. Adding senior living services can raise monthly fees considerably, typically 25% or more. This can be an advantage for those who are interested in and able to pay for such services. But for those neither interested in nor able to afford such an increase, a conversion can trigger a move to a new home.

Age-restricted communities pose particular risks in an era of infectious diseases. If diseases are particularly virulent for older adults, such as is the case with COVID-19, the social element of active adult communities can be significantly curtailed. Further, for rental active adult communities, there may be limited common space to use. It can transform a place that is designed for social connection into one that fosters loneliness.

While the allure of age-restricted housing hinges in large part on the promise of a carefree lifestyle, when considering potential risks and disadvantages, this type of living is certainly not carefree.

EVOLVING OPTIONS

Developers of active adult communities are morphing and adjusting to the shifting tastes of today's older adults. What started exclusively as large-scale for-sale housing communities in the Sunbelt has expanded to include both for-sale and rental options in nearly every market in the country.

Del Webb, now a division of Pulte Homes and one of the largest homebuilders in the country, is an interesting example. They build age-restricted homes in 19 states from the Sunbelt to places to the

Midwest and Northeast. Their offerings include large-scale resort-style communities in typical retirement destinations, like the original Sun City, and options in suburban areas outside of metropolitan centers. The latter scenario provides a solution for people who want to stay where they are or be close to family in the area while maintaining their own space and community. Age-restricted living is becoming less niche and a more common option available in many markets.

At the same time, age-restricted living is emerging as a broader category with active adult communities as a subset. Active adult communities typically provide substantial amenity spaces and programming to promote an active lifestyle. But there are also age-restricted housing options that invest little in amenity space or programming. Their distinction over normal housing is simply that only older adults live there. As a result, there is a growing range of options that fit under the age-restricted living category to help appeal to a broad market.

Policymakers offer financial incentives for developers to build age-restricted housing over conventional options, which creates additional supply. Some municipalities are concerned about new development stressing existing infrastructure, such as roads and schools, and see age-restricted housing as an option to increase tax revenues with only limited incremental costs to the municipality. In areas concerned about overcrowding, zoning restrictions may allow only for age-restricted for-sale homes or rental apartments to be built.

Technology is playing a greater role in active adult communities. Smart home technology is increasingly incorporated into standard and optional designs. In time, technology may also be integrated to help people age safely in their homes. While delivering health care is not something that active adult home builders provide, incorporating technologies to help people stay healthy could be aligned with their core brand and mission.

Affinity-based communities will likely increase. More universities may look to add such housing as a way to diversify their business model. Targeting older adults interested in lifelong learning would be a logical fit. Communities catering to specific ethnic groups are another opportunity. Priya Living, for example, appeals to the Indian community with locations in California and plans to expand nationally.

The lesbian, gay, bisexual, transgender, and queer (LGBTQ) community is a group in need of better housing options. This group can have a hard time integrating seamlessly into mainstream age-restricted housing. Developers are creating dedicated options for this group, recognizing that many in this cohort lack the traditional family or social supports of other groups. Creating specialized communities can provide the needed social connection to age successfully. Palm Springs is a prominent location of innovation in this area.

Another path is for existing age-restricted communities to become better at assimilating LGBTQ residents. I met John at an age-restricted community in Florida. He and his partner wished to downsize and be in a place with older adults. They were concerned about their acceptance as a gay couple. They moved into a large active adult community and were pleasantly surprised by the culture of the community. Given the size of this community—there are about 1,000 residents—they were able to meet other gay couples as well as develop friendships with others in the community, too. The solution for LGBTQ residents may not necessarily be to create niche communities, but to find and help create communities that are inclusive.

Another area worth watching is age-restricted mobile home communities. Once a mom-and-pop industry, age-restricted mobile home communities are increasingly being purchased by institutional investors. These investors are upgrading infrastructure, amenity spaces, and professionalism of operations. At the same time, the quality and design of manufactured homes have improved dramatically in the last decade. Now, high-quality homes, almost unrecognizable as mobile homes, are available for $100,000 or less. Typically, residents purchase a home and lease the underlying land. There are shared spaces, such as pools, gyms, and game rooms, as well as resident programming. This model also works well during a pandemic, as residents have private space in their mobile homes and can socialize in the common spaces when safe.

BEST PRACTICES AND NEXT STEPS

Age-restricted housing is often polarizing: people tend to love it and wish more locations existed, or hate it and suggest it is morally wrong to divide people by age. It is critical to know where you stand on this spectrum. For couples, alignment is particularly important.

It can be helpful to try it before buying it. Fortunately, a number of communities, including The Villages, offer this opportunity officially, and there may be ways to try it informally through a home-sharing service. Narrowing the gap between what you think the experience is and what it actually is will be helpful in either eliminating the option or moving more confidently and excitedly.

Another strategy to consider is to move into an age-restricted community with friends. This has the benefit of starting with an initial community. If you have a cohort of good friends in different locations across the country, this approach could be a way to bring people together. If you plan to move to an age-restricted community within your existing area, moving in with a local friend can help ensure that you see each other more often and ease the transition. This strategy may work particularly well for singles.

For those with means, a home in an active adult community can begin as a second home and eventually transition to a primary home. This approach allows for a more gradual transition, where the second home can be used when the weather is most attractive and then, over time, it can become a home for all seasons.

One thing to be aware of is that the cohort in active adult and age-restricted communities is older than most anticipate. Because a development is designated for people 55 and older doesn't mean that it is made up of primarily 55-year-olds. Average and median ages depend on how long the community has existed and the value proposition of a community. While age ranges can vary significantly, for-sale active adult communities tend to have a median age of people in their 60s, whereas age-restricted apartments tend to have an older median age, typically in the 70s.

CONCLUSION

Age-restricted housing, including rental and for-sale active adult living, is an attractive and growing option for millions of older adults across the country. The choice to live in a vibrant, carefree environment embodies how traditional retirement is viewed. For those interested in a plan for health support as needs arise or who are in immediate need of health services, however, senior living is an important option to consider.

CHAPTER 9

SENIOR LIVING

I like to plan in advance. I moved into Sunrise at Huntcliff Summit, a senior living community in a suburb of Atlanta, in my late 20s. I was the only person under 70 and the only male on my wing. Although an outlier in the community, I made friends, most notably Betty Cobb.

As a solo ager, Betty Cobb was never married, and she was in her early 80s when we met. We were introduced by the administrator of the building, and he forewarned me of her penchant for talking. Yes, she was loquacious, but she was also kind and friendly. We shared a number of meals. I got to hear her story. Several times over.

Betty loved the senior living community. She was healthy, energetic, and outgoing. She made close friends, engaged in the resident programming, and stayed in touch with friends in the neighboring area. She loved the meals, as cooking for one had become tiresome for her. Her living space was small—she lived in a 600-square-foot one-bedroom apartment—but cozy. She made it home. Her status as the de facto mayor of the community was why we were connected.

Betty is a prime example of someone for whom senior living works well. With no family to fall back on, she needed a plan for when her health faded. It is estimated that about 70% of people 65 and older will need long-term care at some point in their lifetime.[1] She wanted to be

RANGE OF SERVICES FOR AGE-RESTRICTED HOUSING AND SENIOR LIVING

	Housing	Activities	Meals	Housekeeping & Laundry	Personal Care Services	Memory Care	Short-Term Care	Long-Term Care
Age-Restricted Housing	■	■						
Independent Living	■	■	■	■				
Assisted Living	■	■	■	■	■	■		
Memory Care	■	■	■	■	■	■		
Skilled Nursing	■	■	■	■	■	■	■	■

Note: Life Plan Communities generally include Independent Living, Assisted Living, and Skilled Nursing all on the same campus.

around others. She wanted to simplify life and had no interest in home maintenance. She also needed a solution that she could afford with her modest savings and pension. Sunrise at Huntcliff Summit checked these boxes in a way that no other type of living option could.

Senior living is a term that encompasses a broad range of living options, including independent living, assisted living, and skilled nursing facilities. Independent living, where Betty resided, includes meals, programming, and housing. Assisted living is similar to independent living but also includes support for activities of daily living (ADLs), such as dressing, bathing, and medication management. In addition, assisted living can have dedicated spaces or buildings for people who have memory loss.

Skilled nursing is health care centric and is divided into two segments: short-term care and long-term care. Short-term care is typically for people exiting a hospital who require additional care for a limited period of time. Examples include rehabilitation for people recovering from heart surgery, strokes, and joint replacements. Short-term care is paid for by Medicare and private insurance. Long-term care is primarily for residents with limited financial resources who qualify for Medicaid. Those with complex long-term care needs and financial resources pay out of pocket for long-term care within skilled nursing; otherwise, most people with financial resources rely on the more homelike setting of assisted living for long-term care needs.

Most senior living communities have a blend of living options. It is most common to have independent living and assisted living paired together. Continuing care retirement communities (CCRCs) typically include independent living, assisted living, and skilled nursing on one campus, with the opportunity for residents to move to higher levels of care as needed. Skilled nursing facilities and dementia care communities are commonly standalone entities.

There is a range of business models. Independent living, assisted living, and skilled nursing are rental properties. There are endowment models, typically for CCRCs, where residents pay a significant one-time fee combined with a monthly fee. This upfront payment, often characterized as an entrance fee, is typically structured in levels of refundability, from 0% (that is, nonrefundable) to 90%, which is refundable upon a move from the community or death. Life plan communities are an endowment model that provides a continuum of care but also bundles in measures of long-term care insurance to provide a predictable monthly fee regardless of the level of care. Because of the breadth of services and the insurance component, life plan communities tend to be the most expensive model. Though much less common, there are also condominium and co-op models that offer a continuum of care.

There is a mix of ownership models. Some communities are owned independently, but institutional investors own the majority of communities, and their market share is increasing. Not-for-profit ownership is significant, particularly among life plan communities. Nonprofit providers have strong reputations for building community and providing quality care.

At the risk of oversimplification, senior living appeals to two groups: older adults who are healthy with a penchant for planning and those with health conditions that require health care services. For the former group, the decision to move into a senior living community tends to be made by the older adult with input from family and advisors. Planners tend to choose CCRCs or independent living communities. Betty is an example of a planner. For the latter group, a health event, such as a fall, or introduction of a chronic condition, like memory loss, can trigger a move. For assisted living and long-term care, a family is generally the decision maker. These two groups are similar in age—the average age for independent living is mid-80s while for assisted living it is late-80s—but different from a health perspective.[2]

ADVANTAGES

Beyond addressing care needs, the biggest advantage is social connection. For many older adults, social and physical isolation have become significant health risks. Family and friends are often more aware of this risk than older adults themselves. With daily meals, programming, and ample space for socialization, it is difficult to *not* get to know other residents in senior living facilities. If anything, the level of social stimulation may be more than introverts are comfortable with. That said, residents are not required to participate in events, and meals can be delivered to rooms, if desired. The option to engage with others regularly and develop friendships stands in contrast to those isolated in a single-family home or apartment.

More than that, senior living can be a place to thrive. The best communities prompt and encourage residents to be stimulated and engaged in life, regardless of health status. Many older adults are subject to ageism and focus on what they can't do. The best senior living communities focus on what residents can do, and celebrate special moments in life and new milestones. In fact, a common refrain among senior living residents is that they wish they had moved sooner, as the lifestyle and impact on their health is better than they imagined.

For planners, senior living scratches the itch: it provides a viable plan for the future. A couple described their decision to move into a life plan community as a "gift to our kids."[3] Their point is an important

one: senior living, particularly life plan communities with the continuum of services and long-term care insurance provisions, can protect
residents from myriad detrimental outcomes, which makes life less
complicated for themselves and their adult children.

My Aunt Dawn and Uncle Rick are planners. A childless middle-
class couple in their 70s, they wanted a viable plan for their future.
After researching options, they relocated from a multistory, single-
family home in Wyoming to their home state of Pennsylvania into a
cottage at a faith-based, not-for-profit life plan community. Owing to
the community's benevolence care fund as well as their savings, they
did not fear of running out of money. They jumped seamlessly into
the social life of the community. Dawn volunteers extensively and has
joined several clubs, including the knitting club. During the coronavirus crisis, she and her friends stitched together dozens of masks for
the community. Rick appreciates his new friends and neighbors but
also wanted a life outside of the senior living community, a desire that
spurred him to work at a deli in town. The new old guy has been a hit
with customers and colleagues, and he has developed intergenerational friendships in the process.

My aunt and uncle illustrate an important point: most planners are
not just looking for a solution to care needs down the road; they are
also looking to find a place where they can thrive in later chapters of
life. Dawn and Rick found community, intellectual simulation, and
new passions. They found opportunities for purpose that enhanced
the lives of those around them. The best senior living communities
focus on enhancing well-being, not just tending to care needs.

Recall Gail from chapter 2. Her story is similar. Without children
and family for support, she was drawn to senior living to have a plan
for care. But she experiences other benefits, too. She makes friends,
particularly among single women and through her Bible study group,
exercises, eats healthy, and has been able to free up time previously
spent maintaining a house.

For adult children, senior living can be an invaluable option in helping manage parents' health. As parents age, the complexity of managing

a loved one's health, particularly if there are multiple chronic conditions such as diabetes, heart disease, and arthritis, can be overwhelming. It is made worse with the challenges in navigating our health system. Partnering with a senior living community to help shoulder the responsibility can be an asset. In the cases of dementia and extreme frailty, senior living may be the only viable option for loved ones to live safely.

The care provided by senior living providers is often very good, compassionate, and increasingly sophisticated. Many providers have mission-based cultures focused on delivering quality care. The best providers attract staff drawn to the impact of their work and retain them by nurturing this calling. As the coronavirus crisis illustrated, hands-on caregiving is essential, and caregivers serve despite the health risks involved. Investments in technology help staff become more efficient and effective, which is particularly important as the complexity of residents' situations increases.

DISADVANTAGES

While one of its advantages is social connection, senior living can be institutionally isolating. Historically, senior living has been separate and apart from the broader community. Its location can be remote, often a function of affordability and availability of land. Senior living communities can require many acres of land, up to 100 acres for the largest-scale developments. Corn fields become senior living developments. Out of sight and out of mind, senior living locations can be forgotten by the greater community.

A remote location furthers a challenge facing many senior living communities: lack of intergenerational interaction. With a lack of young people and an aging resident base, the focus can be on the loss of faculties rather than on celebration of life. The environment can be depressing, sad, and lonely. An architect from Europe once asked the provocative question, "Why do you Americans insist on putting your seniors in ghettos?"[4] Communities that are excellent in providing care can have a sterile culture and lack warmth, akin to a hospital. The result is that some residents in senior living never feel at home.

While care is typically solid within senior living facilities, there are well-documented cases of abuse. This stigma is most associated with skilled nursing but can also be true for assisted living and dementia care. When people are not in a position to look after themselves, they can be targets for bad actors.

Senior living in an era of infectious diseases is particularly problematic. The complexity of managing infectious diseases can be a challenge, and these locations can become hot spots for outbreaks. In such times, communities must protect every resident, potentially limiting or eliminating visitors. As a result, residents can feel even more cut off from the world, including family and friends. The fear of not being with family and friends in one's final days may be reason enough to not choose senior living.

The fear of quarantine in a small apartment and facing greater risk to COVID-19 was the reason that Nicole, a family friend in her early 80s, left her life plan community to move in with family. She had been living in her senior living community for about a year—long enough for her to be friendly with residents but not long enough to form deep friendships. She had relocated from another state, and her ties were with her son and his family in the area. When the coronavirus hit, Nicole and her family feared the worst. Her move-in with her son was an adjustment but better than imagined considering her mild cognitive impairment. Even if her fears were overblown, her move to be with family greatly lessened the risk of contracting the disease and kept her from being separated from loved ones.

Senior living can be prohibitively expensive. There are reasons for the expense: a housing product that includes meals, resident programming, and care requires a lot of people, equipment, and space. For rental independent living, the least involved of service-enriched senior living models, fees range from $2,500 to $5,000 per month, with a median of about $3,000 per month.[5] This compares to about $1,500 for the average rent for an apartment in the United States.[6] Assisted living is more expensive, with a median of about $4,000 per month.[7] This figure can be understated, as care is provided on an à la carte basis depending on health conditions. For memory care, for example, it is common for costs to approach or exceed $10,000 per month. Long-term care in nursing homes is the most expensive. The median yearly cost of a nursing home is in excess of $100,000 per year.[8] Life plan communities require an upfront fee and a monthly service fee. The upfront fee is typically measured in hundreds of thousands of dollars—over $1 million for high-end communities—and monthly fees are in line with or above the range of independent living.

Annual increases can be a challenge, too. In order to be sustainable, providers must at least match the growth of revenue with that of expenses. Since labor is the largest cost for senior living communities and these costs have been rising, monthly fees must rise too, typically 3% to 5% per year. Since monthly fees are high, these annual increases, particularly compounded over a number of years, can put pressure on residents' budgets to the point that some residents may need to move out based on a lack of affordability.

As with other housing options, ownership of senior living matters. Some owners, typically institutional investors, will set pricing based on what the market will bear. This methodology can lead to rent hikes. Other owners, typically not-for-profit providers, may underprice the market. On the surface, this may seem advantageous for residents. But if pricing doesn't support a sustainable business model, there may be future challenges. If, for example, a community underfunds its capital expenditure reserves, the community risks a physical plant that is not attractive to future residents. An inability to attract future residents creates a death spiral for the community, which in turn affects existing residents. Simply put, the right product with the wrong owner can bring anything but peace of mind.

Even though part of senior living's value proposition is to simplify the complexities of aging and deteriorating health, senior living is rarely a turnkey solution for residents and their families. Senior living is not health care. Residents need to continue to advocate for themselves or receive help from family, friends, or third-party health specialists. The best outcomes often involve active engagement at every step. Residents' complex health conditions coupled with high employee turn-over—about a third of staff change each year—make it difficult for communities to be on top of every detail.[9] All things considered, some feel that the cost of senior living does not represent good value given the extra oversight required.

EVOLVING OPTIONS

The field continues to evolve to accommodate the needs and preferences of an aging population. More developers are focusing on sites in walkable urban and suburban locations, which helps to reduce institutional isolation. It is harder to be forgotten if located amidst other parts of the broader community. A centralized location allows residents to venture more easily venture into the broader community and is also more convenient for visitors.

A location strategy close to the broader community adds opportunities for intergenerational interaction. Some developers are even integrating into non-age-restricted environments. Merrill Gardens is a leading senior living developer and operator in the Pacific Northwest. They developed and operate Merrill Gardens at the University, an assisted living and independent living community, adjacent to a non-age-restricted apartment project that caters to graduate students and young faculty. The retirement community's dining room is open to residents of both buildings. As a result, multiple generations get to know each other over meals. More developers and operators are looking to create amenity spaces open to the community around them.

A number of existing senior living communities are adding inter-generational elements. Judson Smart Living is a provider of senior living services in Cleveland, Ohio, that has placed an emphasis on inter-generational interactions. Their downtown location creates structured opportunities for preschool- to college-age students to interact with residents in the community. At the same time, Judson residents are active in the community by volunteering at schools, engaging with local community groups, and mentoring youth. What makes Judson particularly unusual is that they have established a relationship with the Cleveland Institute of Music, whereby students are provided complimentary lodging in exchange for regular musical performances. By living intergenerationally, residents young and old are able to have regular interactions and form genuine friendships. Older adults hail that the dynamic makes them feel younger, and the students have described it as "life-changing."[10]

Another trend is the colocation of senior living communities on or near college campuses. In some cases, like The Vi at Palo Alto, California, located near Stanford University, a community exists on leased or purchased land of a university, but no formal relationship exists otherwise. In other cases, like Lasell Village at Lasell University in Newton, Massachusetts, the relationship and commitment to life-long learning are so strong that residents are required to enroll in classes. These types of senior living communities are scattered across the country and tend to appeal to people who value education and want to be close to the vibe of a college campus. University-based senior living is an example of affinity living, where people are drawn to live together based on shared interests. Other examples include locations oriented to LGBTQ residents, creative arts, and veterans, among others.

There is a push to create more affordable senior living options, particularly those targeting middle-market consumers. While these new concepts are in their infancy, the fundamental idea is to unbundle services and rely more on technology, on-demand service delivery, and integrated health care to provide services when needed to keep people healthy. This approach decreases fixed costs and, more importantly, the size of the workforce. Affordable senior living will be a key area of growth in the coming decades.

Looking to appeal to healthy boomers, senior living facilities, life plan communities in particular, are broadening their range of programming and activities to focus on well-being. Gone are the days of playing bingo nightly. Instead, resources are employed to help residents explore what they want their next chapter to look like. Life coaches and educational curriculums are utilized. Common spaces are designed to foster resident collaboration in flexible ways; it is not just about creating a woodshop for the men and a crafts room for the women. Fitness rooms are stocked with contemporary equipment and knowledgeable instructors. Unit floorplans account for the likelihood of staying involved in the work world, including allocating space for a home office. Community portals and other technology investments are made to help facilitate connections in and outside of the community.

Some communities are doubling down on resident engagement. Rather than treat residents as hospital patients or hotel guests, these communities consider their residents to be citizens. In this model, residents are empowered to create a community where they are connected to and look out for each other. They drive and shape culture more so than management or ownership. Such communities have active participation in resident-led clubs and a direct say in governance through empowered resident councils.

One such community is Horizon House, a not-for-profit life plan community in the Northwest. Its value proposition rests primarily on its resident-driven culture. It is a beehive of activity, most of which is led by residents, not staff. It has about 400 independent living units with 45 resident-led committees and 23 activities led by resident facilitators. Each resident participates in more than a dozen activities per month on average. It seems to be working: 95% of residents would recommend Horizon House, and the community has amassed a waiting list of prospective residents.[11]

Resident empowerment may be the future for senior living. Jill Vitale-Aussem, an executive in the senior living industry and author of *Disrupting the Status Quo of Senior Living: A Mindshift*, sees a major shift in approach for senior living. According to Jill, "Innovative organizations are realizing that reframing residents as citizens rather than customers promotes self-efficacy, meaningful purpose and a strong sense of belonging—all of which are essential to well-being."[12]

Innovations are happening on the care side of senior living. As dementia has become increasingly common among older adults, assisted living developers and operators have created dedicated dementia-focused buildings and programming. These communities are thoughtfully designed for safety and socialization, and programming is created specifically for those with memory impairment and is delivered by trained staff. Though expensive, these dementia-focused communities allow residents to thrive in a way that a normal assisted living does not.

Technology is gaining a greater role in senior living. Technology, notably telehealth, is allowing residents to receive health care services without leaving their community. It is also helping some residents stay in low-care environments by delivering health services to the resident, rather than requiring the resident to relocate to higher levels of care. Technology is helping residents stay in communication with loved ones outside of the community as well as build community among residents.

BEST PRACTICES AND NEXT STEPS

Before considering senior living for you or loved ones, it is important to understand where you stand. This perspective is multifaceted: you must consider health and finances as well as legal and life goals. This work can be done on your own or within the family, but working with professionals can be valuable. If you are a healthy and a planner, doing this work will help identify the right type of senior living community. Independent living or a life plan community is the likely fit. If planning for a loved one with care needs, finding the best care setting can be a challenge, particularly if the decision is urgent. It is hard to plan on someone else's behalf, but having a plan before a health event occurs can be enormously valuable in order to make important decisions on a tight time line. Research shows that the gap between where people would prefer to age and where they end up living often arise from a lack of planning.[13]

Financial considerations may be the most important. Senior living is expensive, even for those with the foresight to purchase long-term care insurance. It is easy to be optimistic each step of the way. We may neither truly appreciate the severity of a loved one's condition nor their likely progression. Optimism is not your friend in planning; it can lead to bad decisions that trigger subsequent moves to other communities and facilities. Any physical move by older adults poses a risk. The goal is to be conservative and account for a range of contingencies.

When choosing a community, it is critical to understand the dynamics of the ownership group and management company. Long-term owners can be attractive, as the risk of turnover of key staff is lessened. The long tenure of staff, particularly care staff, can be the key to a community's success. Long-term owners include real estate investment trusts (REITs) and private investment groups. Short-term investment groups can come in many forms, but private equity firms in particular generally sell investments within a five- to seven-year period.

It is important to get a feel for the financial stability of a community. This research is particularly important for endowment communities because residents could be at risk of losing their initial payment, often measured in hundreds of thousands of dollars. Even if residents don't lose their funds, financial challenges can lead to an erosion in the quality of services and care. Financial disclosures are provided or can be requested. The financials of life plan communities can be complicated and may require the help of a financial professional to understand them.

Management companies are also important to research. Large management companies have the benefit of scale and sophisticated systems. But the attention given to a community can get lost amidst a company's other priorities. Conversely, a management company with few communities may lack sophistication and professionalism. Sometimes, the best communities are ones with enough scale to attract quality leaders and invest in necessary infrastructure but small enough to make sure that each community gets attention from corporate staff. From this perspective, strong regional operators may be the best option.

While a management company matters, the executive director is critical. Getting time with the executive director can be a key step in the decision-making process. It is important to get a sense of the leader's set of experiences, leadership style, and commitment. For some executive directors, a community may be a stepping-stone to greater responsibilities, and a change may be around the corner.

For healthy older adults, fit and timing are critical. A senior living community will become your new home where you may live in for many years. Get a feel for the culture of the community, and understand that it may be dictated by residents more than anything else. Time spent visiting with residents over meals or participating in programming can help you get a feel for how things really are, not just how they are characterized by the marketing department. Also, it is best to move while you are still healthy, which will allow you to best integrate into the community and make friends. A common refrain for those who choose to move into life plan communities is that they wished they had done so earlier.

When looking for recommendations, word of mouth is often the most helpful. Online reviews can be skewed by a few negative experiences with staff no longer at the community or propped up by efforts to motivate residents to share positive reviews. Referral services, like A Place for Mom, can be deceiving, as they may only refer you to communities from which they receive a commission.

Skilled nursing bears special mention. Skilled nursing offers a particularly broad range of quality both in terms of quality of care and the built environment. A number of skilled nursing companies and locations are highly leveraged with minimal capital to make changes. There was a building boom of skilled nursing facilities starting in the 1960s, and unfortunately, a number of the buildings still look from that time period. The federal government has created a five-star rating system to help consumers evaluate and compare options. Unfortunately, it is a rating system that is still evolving and there is a time delay in the data, so one should not be too confident in a community's rating. There are five-star-rated facilities where I would never consider sending a loved one and three-star-rated facilities that I consider to be excellent. It is best to review the data from Centers for Medicare and

Medicaid Services (CMS) and other sources, but ask for a specific set of recommendations from the hospital, typically from the discharge planner, and the rationale behind those recommendations. Many hospitals outline a preferred list of providers based on objective data to help consumers sort the wheat from the chaff among skilled nursing locations.

Particularly in light of the health risks posed by the coronavirus and influenza, infection control is something that any community should take seriously. Be sure to ask how infection control is handled and what measures are in place to help stave off outbreaks. You might also consider asking for a recent history. Third-party measures of effective infection control are lacking. Resources exist for skilled nursing facilities,[14] but less so for private-pay senior living, such as independent living and assisted living. States provide oversight for assisted living, and some states maintain data to share with consumers. For example, during the pandemic, Maryland created a COVID-19 dashboard for congregate facility settings, including skilled nursing and assisted living.[15] This tool helped consumers make informed decisions based on up-to-date data.

CONCLUSION

Senior living is better than many realize. The media, particularly during challenging times like the coronavirus crisis, tends to focus on situations where things go wrong. As a whole, however, people's experience with senior living is positive, and residents appreciate the care and desire to serve embodied in staff. Some residents describe the decision to move into senior living as one of the best decisions of their lives. It certainly was for Betty Cobb.

Unfortunately, it is an option that relatively few can afford. It can also be one that simply doesn't resonate. As a result, other innovative models are emerging.

CHAPTER 10

EMERGING OPTIONS, FROM COHOUSING TO TINY HOMES

Many people are searching for better housing options that will help them thrive as they age. Innovative approaches often incorporate lower cost, enhanced social connection, improved design, integrated technology, or some combination of these characteristics. It is unclear which new models will gain popularity and scale, and which will fail to get traction. One thing is for sure: with a growing and more diverse population of older adults, with continued longevity gains and additional technology breakthroughs, the introduction of innovative housing models will be a constant in the years ahead.

HOME SHARING

Sometimes, innovations can be a rendition of an old model. Take *The Golden Girls*, the iconic sitcom from the '80s. The plot is predicated on four older single women (three widows and one divorcée) sharing a house in Miami. The owner of the house, Blanche, posts an ad and attracts Rose (played by Betty White) and Dorothy. Dorothy brings along her 80-year-old mother, Sophia. The housing situation saves everyone money, and more importantly, it gains everyone a friend as emphasized by the theme song, "Thank You for Being a Friend."

Today, the tools for finding a roommate are more sophisticated.

Wendi Burkhardt is the founder of SilverNest, an online roommate matchmaking service for older adults. After her father passed away, she saw her mom struggle with loneliness and maintaining a single-family house. Her mom didn't want to move, but Wendi knew her situation wasn't ideal. Wendi thought having a roommate could be a solution, but finding a match was difficult. This experience was Wendi's inspiration to start the online platform.

Online roommate matchmaking services work. First, they attract a pool of interested parties, including homeowners. They screen for fit to enhance the odds of a successful match. They create an easy process for homeowners to create a lease, set up automatic rent payments, and provide best practices for home sharing. The *Today Show* showcased two women who used the service: Eileen, a 70-something single homeowner, and Jean, a 55-year-old recent divorcee.[1] Jean could afford to live on her own but didn't want to be isolated. Eileen had friends but found living alone lonely and would benefit from supplemental income. Both had needs from time to time that could be aided by a roommate, providing relief from leaning too much on friends and family. In their case, the living situation didn't infringe on either woman's lifestyle and created a means to support each other.

Such matchmaking services are available not just for peers but across generations, too. Brenda Atchinson is a celebrity in my circles. Her picture has been prominently featured in several publications, and she has been interviewed countless times. She uses a roommate matchmaking service called Nesterly to link to students as roommates. This is intergenerational roommate matchmaking. It's an arrangement that resonates: solve a housing affordability issue for students while producing an additional revenue stream for older adults and creating intergenerational connections.

Single and in her 60s, Brenda lives in the Roxbury neighborhood of Boston. She's been living there for more than 30 years, but her townhome has been there substantially longer—since the 1800s. It is beautiful, but it requires a lot to maintain—both inside and outside—and it is costly to keep warm during harsh winters. She realized that to make things work, she could benefit from an extra pair of hands. She needed a roommate.

At the same time, Boston is crawling with students with its collection of universities. As the area has grown, however, the housing supply has not increased in step, and housing costs have skyrocketed. Students, particularly graduate students, are caught in a bind, needing to be close to their university but having few affordable options.

Brenda has roomed with various students over the past several years, and the experience has exceeded her expectations. Since becoming a host, it is hard for her to imagine continuing to live in her home alone. In exchange for an affordable guest room, roommates are expected to take out the trash, rake leaves, shovel snow, and perform other sundry tasks around the house. It has been fun for everyone, and her roommates have been independent, respectful, and handy. She's been able to share her culture, music, and culinary delights with young people hailing from as far away as Greece. Preparing and sharing meals, tending to the garden together, and fixing up the house have created a natural bond between her and various roommates. She's even attended the graduation ceremonies of roommates. Technically, Brenda is just sharing her home. But with her positive energy and loving spirit, the reality is that she has created lifelong connections and made a considerable impact on the lives of young adults.[2]

Home sharing is expected to grow. As the market of interested people and homeowners expands, the ability to make good matches should improve. As more people have satisfying experiences and word spreads, it will be more socially acceptable to share a home. One of the advantages is the low commitment required. If it doesn't work as you expect, you can always revert back to your previous living situation. If you try it and like it, you may not want to go back. You could be the next Brenda.

COHOUSING AND CO-LIVING

Like home sharing, cohousing is not a new model. It has been around thousands of years, but today it offers a different twist, particularly for older adults. Cohousing is an intentional community centered on shared values and shared spaces while simultaneously creating measures for personal privacy. It's like living as a tribe. Practically speaking, it involves common spaces surrounded by private homes. Group spaces typically include a common kitchen and dining room, laundry and recreational areas, and outdoor spaces, like group gardens and pathways. Parking is generally on the perimeter, with homes facing each other and shared spaces in the center. It is designed for community building and spontaneous interactions.

The core of cohousing is living in relationship. Neighbors play together, cook for each other, share resources, and work collaboratively. Common property is managed and maintained by members of the community, providing ample opportunities for engagement. It's almost like living with chosen family. The proximity and shared decision making cultivate a culture of sharing, caring, and developing close relationships.

Developments are on the smaller side, typically ranging from 20 to 40 units. Most cohousing models are structured as condominiums where members own their single-family house and have an ownership stake in the common spaces. Housing units are small, to encourage more time spent in the common areas. All else equal, living in a cohousing development is less expensive than its single-family equivalent because the ethos of helping and sharing minimizes the need for equipment and tools of your own, as well as for third-party service providers, such as for child care or companion services.

The majority of the 300 cohousing communities in the United States are intergenerational. Given supportive culture that helps build strong relationships, the environment can be particularly conducive for older adults to support the needs of young families and vice versa. This dynamic can create surrogate grandparent and grandchild relationships.

Cohousing can be created with older adults in mind through design elements and expectations set by bylaws, including age restriction. The advantage of this approach is that housing units and common spaces are more likely to employ universal design features and ensure the environment is accessible and safe for those with limited mobility. Space can be designed with anticipation of live-in caregiving support, perhaps shared across a number of residents.

People who live in cohousing communities are passionate about living in community. Sometimes, that's not enough. Only about one-third of groups that look to start a cohousing community are able to make it a reality. Complications abound, ranging from finding afford-able land to securing city permits to attracting sufficient interest. Even those that make it into existence find that life in a cohousing commu-nity is not as idyllic as they envisioned. Also, because each cohousing community is unique and has a strong culture, selling a unit can be challenging because fit is critical for all parties involved.

There are derivatives of the cohousing model. A comparatively sim-ple one is where couples come together to create a house or cluster of housing on their own to age together. Substantial effort is required, but not to the same degree as in a traditional cohousing development. In this model, good friends can collect from various geographies, map out a plan to live together, and take care of each other over time. This model can be more complicated than it seems. Participants need to think carefully about contingencies and responsibilities for when health fades. You need to be careful to avoid risks of overburdening residents, particularly if participants move out either for higher levels of care or because of financial challenges.

Co-living is another spin on cohousing. It is a new approach to communal living focused on millennials, but it has appealed to old-er adults, too. Co-living is a rental model that has small units offset with ample community spaces and regular resident programming. The units are typically quite small—microunits can be less than 200 square feet—and come furnished. Co-living is available largely in urban areas where reasonably priced housing is hard to find.

Its DNA is similar to cohousing in that it attracts residents that have a shared set of interests and values. Being part of a community is cen-tral. It's different in several ways, however. The community between residents is cultivated by a professional host versus occurring organically among residents. Relying on a professional management company can help smooth out edges and dynamics between residents, but it also introduces a profit-motivated third party. A rental model makes it easier to leave if it is not right for you; however, ease of change can lead to higher resident turnover, making it difficult to build lasting friendships. It's unclear how appealing co-living in its current state will be for older adults, particularly when units are so small, but its evolution may hit a sweet spot, particularly in suburban areas allowing for larger units that can appeal to a broader swath of the aging demographic.

INTENTIONAL INTERGENERATIONAL LIVING COMMUNITIES

A place to live can also serve as a platform for serving others. Intentional intergenerational living communities are akin to cohousing in the sense that they build an authentic community. However, they demand more of residents. These communities tackle challenging intergenerational problems, such as assisting foster care youth and their families, and they do so by an all-in commitment for those involved.

An example of an intentional intergenerational living community is the Treehouse Foundation, an organization founded by Judy Cockerton. In her late 40s, Judy persuaded her husband to foster kids. The experience opened her eyes to the pressing needs of foster youth and opportunities for people, especially older adults, to come alongside them to spend time with, mentor, and love them. This inspired her to create the Treehouse Community in Easthampton, Massachusetts, about 100 miles west of Boston. The community has more than 100 residents ranging in age from babies to older adults in their 90s and includes 12 family homes and 48 one-bedroom cottages designed for older adults. Supported by social services staff, community members interact daily with kids in a wide range of activities, with no purpose greater than to show that they are cared for. The impact on youth has been remarkable, particularly as compared to outcomes typical for foster children, and it has been highly rewarding for the older residents.

Few intentional intergenerational living communities exist, but more are coming. Beyond its impact on youth and older adults, housing is more affordable for older adults because rent is subsidized to compensate for their investment in youth. This housing model is for those dedicated to service, and it may be a clever way to match passion for a cause with a need for housing and community.

COOPERATIVE LIVING

Cooperative living, or co-ops, for older adults is another model that is growing, albeit slowly. Community involvement is important and is reflected in the ownership structure. Members purchase a fractional share in the community, which includes the ability to deduct their portion of property taxes and mortgage interest, and share the responsibilities of ownership within an organization controlled by its members. Co-ops can have a mix of single-family houses and apartments along with common space for gathering and programming. Age-restricted co-ops can be akin to active adult communities with no health care services, though there are co-ops that offer a continuum of care.

I have worked with several age-restricted co-ops, including The Village at Duxbury in Duxbury, Massachusetts, an hour south of Boston. The Village of Duxbury offers a mix of garden homes, independent living apartments, and assisted living. It's beautiful and well managed, but what sets it apart is the residents' engagement and desire to sustain an excellent community. Working with the board of directors, I have been impressed with the commitment of resident board members to make their community as strong as possible for current and future residents. It's not as surprise that resident satisfaction is high.

There are about 125 age-restricted co-ops in the country, with a noticeable cluster in the Midwest. These communities are particularly appealing to middle-market older adults, in part because of a culture that keeps monthly costs low with minimal annual increases. Resident owners have a greater influence on key decisions than traditional senior living residents; while there is a strong sense of community, it does not require the level of commitment of cohousing.

TINY HOMES AND ACCESSIBLE DWELLING UNITS

Over the past 40 years, the average home in the United States has increased in size by more than 1,000 square feet, essentially doubling the amount of living space per person over this period. In recent years, however, a counter trend has emerged. A subset of people is moving into smaller houses, in some cases much smaller houses.

Sarah Susanka, architect and author of the *Not So Big House* series, is a pioneering voice for this movement.[3] I stumbled across her book in the late '90s, and it had a strong impact on me. She highlights quality over quantity—why not create fewer but better spaces?—and outlines a philosophy of creating spaces that are of human scale. She emphasizes size, lighting, design, and other techniques to make spaces inviting, usable, and joyful.

Tiny homes take these concepts and implement them at a microscale. Tiny homes can be as small as 80 square feet or as large as 700 square feet, though the range tends to be between 100 to 400 square feet, or about 250 square feet per occupant. These tiny homes can resemble studio apartments, are crafted in a variety of styles, and can be customized to a variety of tastes. They are typically one story, though some take advantage of loft spaces, and often incorporate universal design principles. They are energy efficient and thoughtful about the use of every square foot. Modular systems can allow for a greater degree of flexibility, particularly in instances where there are no internal load-bearing walls.

Tiny homes have resonated with older adults. Roughly two of five tiny homeowners are 50 years of age or older. One reason is financial. Tiny homes cost as little as $10,000, with an average cost of about $23,000, an attractive alternative to other housing options. As a result, owners of tiny houses are more likely to own their home outright (68%) as compared to US homeowners at large (29%). Utility costs and maintenance costs are low, too. This lifestyle can be freeing. For those able to downsize to this degree, more energy can be focused on life outside the home. These homes can appeal to someone's sense of independence and choice, and serve as a viable alternative to traditional apartment-style senior living, particularly when integrated as part of a broader community.

Tiny homes designed for the needs of older adults have been described as "granny pods." In 2010, a Methodist minister from Virginia partnered with the Virginia Tech Research Center in Blacksburg, Virginia, to create the MEDCottage.[4] Their prototype is 12 by 24 feet, or about 300 square feet, and has vinyl siding, double French doors (to accommodate a wheelchair and hospital equipment), and looks like a small bungalow. It has safety features like hand railings, defibrillators, first aid supplies, lighted floorboards, and a soft floor to minimize injury from falls. It also incorporates interactive video and devices that monitor vital signs, such as blood pressure and blood glucose, and transmit real-time readings to caregivers and physicians. Adoption of granny pods to the level of the MEDCottage has been limited, but it provides a flavor of what's possible with design, technology, and health care integration. In addition, Dr. Bill Thomas, a serial innovator in the aging field, has created MINKA, a company that utilizes a proprietary robotic process to print tiny homes on a development site within *weeks*. The right models have the potential to scale rapidly.

Tiny homes and nanny pods are part of the larger movement around accessible dwelling units, or ADUs. ADUs can vary widely in cost and purpose. Their use can be a strategy to create additional and more affordable housing, which is particularly valuable in markets with a housing crunch. If designed flexibly, these dwellings create options. They can be used for visitors and aging family or rented for income. For an older adult, adding an ADU could create a home-sharing opportunity.

Think back to Bob from chapter 2. He decides to stay put in his single-family house in Southern California. With financial support from his family, he adds an ADU that includes universal design features and has the flexibility to be his primary dwelling in the future. He rents the ADU to a young professional, but he could use it for home sharing to have a friend nearby. Bob created options: he can rent the ADU and live in the house, rent the house and live in the ADU, or rent both to help pay for long-term care elsewhere. If he wanted to live with family, a family member could come live with him, and each party would have privacy.

The broader ADU movement is catching on, particularly as more municipalities allow such development. This is good news for older adults, as it will create more housing options. Carmel, Indiana, a small city north of Indianapolis, is considering changes to code to make the development of ADUs possible.[5] Resident Janet Chilton is excited about the prospect of ADUs in Carmel. At 68 years old, Janet is not interested in moving into senior living and would like to live in community. "My family all moved away. I thought about moving to Colorado, but the idea of picking up and moving far away is daunting," she says. "This is where I live. This is where my friends are." Living in an ADU may make her vision possible.

ADUs are something for adult children to consider. When my family and I purchased our house, part of the draw was a spot in the backyard to develop an ADU in the future. Depending on the circumstances of our parents and other aging family members, having such a dwelling could be important.

CONCLUSION

From home sharing to cohousing and co-living to intentional intergenerational living communities to cooperative living to tiny homes and accessible dwelling units, it is encouraging to see innovations creating additional living options for older adults. As most of these ideas are new and haven't hit the market at scale, we don't yet know the true advantages and disadvantages of each model. We can expect more models to enter the market in the years and decades ahead.

CHAPTER 11

LIVING WITH OR NEAR FAMILY

In the Oscar-nominated film *Avalon*, the Krichinsky family immigrates from Eastern Europe to America in waves starting in the early 1900s. The movie takes place in the late 1940s and early 1950s, with extended family of grandparents, aunts, uncles, and scores of grandchildren clustered in adjacent row homes in Baltimore. It's a close-knit group that does everything together, prioritizing family, tradition, and community over individual preferences. They hold family councils and pool money for charitable giving, including helping extended family in need. Thanksgiving is a family tradition where dozens of family members come together, and the din of laughter and shouting is deafening.

But times change. The younger generation seeks economic opportunity and succeeds, living out the American dream. Members of the family move to the suburbs, separating their nuclear families from the herd. Trying to fit in further, younger family members shed some of their heritage, including changing their last name to seem more American. The once close family frays to the point where Thanksgiving celebrations with extended family are replaced by a TV tray dinner for each nuclear family. The story closes with the patriarch wondering how it all happened as he lives alone and isolated from family in a long-term care facility. He laments, "In the end, you spend everything you've ever saved, sell everything you've ever owned, just to exist in a place like this."

The story of the Krichinsky family is sensationalized by Hollywood, but it is a thread that exposes a truth of our society at large: over the years and for a variety of reasons, we have increasingly traded ties and obligations to support extended family for personal mobility and autonomy. This is not to say this trade is necessarily a bad one—this mobility has fueled unparalleled economic opportunity for decades—but it has implications and consequences.

Your story may or may not parallel that of the Krichinsky family, but there's an important threshold question for each of us to consider: What role does extended family have in my plan for aging? For adult children and extended family, the question is, What expectation do loved ones have of me to support them as they age?

WHY FAMILY?

For some, either through cultural expectations or economic necessity, living with family is the default. During the coronavirus epidemic, I signed up to be a phone buddy for an older adult in my area. I was matched with Phil, a widower in his mid-70s who recently relocated from Northeast to move in with his daughter's family in Texas. Previously, Phil spent his entire life in the same town working in a regional post office for the US Postal Service. He worked for the agency for more than 50 years. When his wife passed away, he determined the best option was to relocate to live with family. He misses friends, but he is close to his grandchildren and has built-in support. This setup will help him save money for long-term care should he need it.

For others, the decision may be borne out of opportunity and mutual benefit. My friend Bethany and her husband have a young child and decided to relocate to live with her parents. They moved from an urban setting to a rural one and bought and remodeled a house together, making accommodations for private and shared spaces. It wasn't something either party needed to do, but everyone believed in the benefits of a move. Several years in, the move has worked well.

Professional opportunities have been harder to find, but the lower cost of living and time with family has been worth it. For Bethany's parents, they have built-in support as they age; for Bethany and her husband, they don't have to look far to find a babysitter.

A key reason for living close to family is for grandparents to be involved in the lives of grandchildren and them in the lives of their grandparents. Being present in grandchildren's lives can be rewarding and creates a foundation for a solid, ongoing relationship. It allows for participation in large events, such as graduations, but also in the smaller but frequent gatherings, such as sports, concerts, and birthday parties.

Proximity can allow grandparents to fill in gaps for parents. A family friend, Brian, lives close to his grandchildren and for years took on the role of lead baseball coach for his grandson Sean. His son-in-law, Steve, would have loved to coach his son, but he didn't have the time because his work was too demanding. Brian had the time and skills. He was all in. He led multiple weekly practices and traveled near and far for games. Energetic and good natured, Brian is perfect as a coach for Little Leaguers. He became a neighborhood celebrity and was written up in the local papers. This level of engagement for a grandfather with his grandchildren can be described as intergenerational fatherhood.

In other situations, grandparents can play a key role in making daily life work. Grandparents can fill key roles like regular childcare, babysitting, and tutoring. Shuttling kids to and from after school commitments can be a full-time job, and grandparents can share the load. Proximity allows grandparents to get involved in their grandchildren's school, helping not only their kin but other kids as well. A friend's mom, who works part-time, volunteers every Friday at her grandchildren's public school and is a key asset in the classroom. Teachers know her on a first-name basis, as do many of the kids. Not only is she able to see her grandchildren regularly and help them, but she also models volunteering and community involvement for everyone.

Still, for others, the decision to live with family may be due to an immediate need for help. My friend Jim faced an important decision during the early stages of the coronavirus crisis. His mom was living in a nearby senior living community, and he and other family members were concerned about her safety and the impact of sheltering in place alone in a small apartment. He decided to help out and gained a new but well-known roommate for months. Such a move can have significant implications, particularly if there are caregiving responsibilities required.

WHY NOT FAMILY?

Living with or by family may not be a wise decision for a host of reasons. Some cases are simple: there's not a relationship. The idea of living with or near family does not evoke positive emotions for everyone. In these cases, it may be best to see family every so often and lean more heavily on other social networks for support and enjoyment.

Living close to family may require more of older adults and their families than either party is willing to assume. Older adults may have social and health needs that are beyond what family members are able or skilled to meet. At the same time, families with young children can come with a lot of needs. Grandparents can get caught in the vortex of their adult children's lives and sucked into regular responsibilities that don't align with how they would like to spend their time. Grandparents can feel taken advantage of as unpaid laborers.

Location can be an issue. You may find that while you love your children and grandchildren, you can't imagine relocating to where they live. Maybe your family lives in a cold part of the country and you're desperate for warm weather, or the cost of living for an area where family lives is prohibitive for the type of lifestyle you would like to have.

Location can be a moving target. Depending on career path and ambitions, adult children may not be in a fixed spot. Opportunities may take them from place to place, and if you are committed to being with them, you would need to follow them as they move. Even when family has established roots, if the opportunity of a lifetime presents itself, adult children may not adequately consider the disruption a move may cause in your life.

If relocating is required to be closer to family, losing existing support networks is a key consideration. If you have lived in a place for decades and feel rooted, changing to a new environment is difficult in and of itself. If a move is driven principally by the desire to be close to family and the expectation is to be intertwined in their lives, building a similar support and friend structure may be difficult. You may be trading a good situation for a bad one.

The COVID-19 pandemic exposed an unexpected risk of intergenerational living. In times of infectious diseases, viruses can spread from young family members to vulnerable elders. It is believed that part of what led to a spike in pandemic-related deaths in New York City was the high percentage of multigenerational families living under one roof.[1]

MANAGING EXPECTATIONS

If the decision is to live near or with family, a key element for success is managing expectations. If living near family is not new, there will be a track record of what does and doesn't work. If there are things that don't work, bring these issues up and talk about what can change to make things better. If you live near family with whom you are considering moving in, or you do not currently live near family and are considering moving to be with or near family, laying out expectations and ground rules can be important so that no one is left disappointed.

These conversations should occur in advance of a significant change or move, but sometimes circumstances don't allow for that. For example, a friend's mother relocated from the suburbs to the city to be close to her daughter, son-in-law, and grandchildren. Everyone was excited about the change and opportunity for frequent interaction, as well as help with the young children. The tension was with the frequency. Her mom wanted to see family almost daily, a high level of interaction that was too cumbersome for my friend's family. They discussed the gap in expectations and arrived at a weekly shared meal along with other opportunities to engage with grandchildren at their school. This was an important compromise.

My brother-in-law, Dr. Henry Cloud, is a psychologist and expert in managing family dynamics. His popular book *Boundaries* recommends being honest with yourself and your needs before agreeing to family requests.[2] Without proper boundaries for all parties involved, any situation with family is bound to face inevitable conflicts or disappointments.

VARIETY OF OPTIONS

There are plenty of housing options for people who wish to incorporate elements of family in their lives. Some of them involve living *with* family, while others allow for living *near* family. For those who don't live close to family, there is an opportunity to be intentional about creating time for meaningful and extended connection when together.

The most obvious scenario is to live with family. This can happen in the context where older adults move in with family or vice versa. These situations can be complicated because one party is entering another's space. The hosting party is used to a certain environment that changes with the introduction of roommates. Neither party may be used to sharing spaces at this point in their life, and it requires an adjustment for all involved.

Physical changes may also be part of the adjustment. Some minor changes may include rearranging or swapping bedrooms to better align with needs and preferences. More significant adjustments akin to a house remodel might also be needed. Changes may be required for entryways, bathrooms, and other spaces to make them more accommodating for the range of needs of family members. It may involve a house expansion to create an extra room, or other features could be needed. It may not be a small undertaking.

Some alternative models allow for living with family without 24-7 interaction. A good example is from the prior chapter: the use of accessible dwelling units. ADUs create private space for the occupant and allow for interaction in the main house.

Another option is to buy, build, or renovate to create a home designed for intergenerational living. Several home builders have created models and layouts that are designed specifically for extended families to live together. These designs create private and shared spaces all under one roof. While one can build or renovate such a home as well, there can be potentially more headaches and higher costs in doing so. If taking on such a project, it is wise to use architects and contractors with experience in this domain.

A less common model, partly because it can be difficult to pull off, is to live adjacent to or on the same street with family. This approach allows for separate spaces and the ability to see each other on a planned as well as spontaneous basis. At most, family is a short walk away. This scenario happened with a friend and his parents as much through serendipity as planning. His parents relocated to the area and happened upon a house behind his. After discussion, all parties felt that such a move would be advantageous. After more than 15 years, the situation has worked well. The grandparents have been actively engaged in the lives of their grandchildren, and the nearness has provided a form of security for all.

With people living longer, some unexpected scenarios are emerging. Senior living communities haven begun to see more families of multiple generations living together. Historically, this has happened because the typical ordinance of a retirement community is to have one occupant of 55 or older as a resident, which allowed an age-qualified resident to have their grandchild live with them, for example. What's different now is that members qualify by age though they are from different generations. I first saw this at a downtown Chicago life plan community where a mother and daughter were roommates. The mother was in her 90s and the daughter in her 60s. They were able to support each other while building community in and outside of the retirement community. As we collectively live longer and are subject to episodic health events, it's not just aging parents that may need help; more and more adult children will be older adults that need support, and they may look to their parents for assistance.

Another approach is to live near but not with family. This is the default for families that already live in the same area. Under this scenario, housing options are broad. It is important to recognize the trade-offs, however, when a certain location is fixed. For example, the range of senior living options may be more limited, particularly those that are within a 15-minute drive to family, than housing options more broadly. There may be some compromises for a home in order to be in reasonable proximity to family.

There's another risk: busyness. In our distracted and harried age, time can slip away. Families with overscheduled calendars can find it hard to make time to see others, including family. It's not necessarily a one-way street. As older adults get enmeshed in various social circles, they, too, can be hard to reach. There's some truth to the adage that people have never been busier than when they retire.

Distance is a key variable to consider. We can all fall victim to the "out of sight, out of mind" reality. The frequency of getting together is lessened by distance, and that relationship is not necessarily linear. Living 5 minutes versus 20 minutes apart may result in seeing each other more than four times as often. But distance is not the only measure. Having locations that integrate nicely into the flow of life, living close to a grocery store or the gym, will likely result in more interactions than a location that requires a single-purpose visit. Also consider traffic patterns. The prospect of bad traffic can be enough to deter a visit.

When family doesn't live close by, you have to be creative to see loved ones often enough for meaningful social connection. Sharing holidays is a common strategy, though these periods aren't necessarily the most relaxed or conducive for connection, particularly on a one-on-one basis. Spending regular vacations together can help. Each year, my wife's extended family spends a week together. It can be hard to pull off when coordinating about 20 schedules, but the tradition has enabled friendships to flourish across generations.

None of my grandparents lived close to our family growing up. Through a clever arrangement, however, my mom's parents housesat for our neighbors for one month each summer. As a result, I was able to spend substantial time with my maternal grandparents. We played games, took hikes, retold family stories, and shared meals together. It was a nice compromise for all involved.

ROLE FOR FAMILY WHEN HEALTH FADES

Some of life's circumstances may require more family involvement than others. When we're in good health, living with or near family can be valuable but not necessary. But when health deteriorates, particularly into our 70s and beyond, having family nearby can be a lifeline.

When health fades, living far from family can be particularly challenging. Anxieties increase for an older adult and their family, especially if the older adult lives in a suboptimal housing situation. There's so much that can go wrong. Being apart makes it hard to understand what risks a particular situation presents. For adult children, it can raise an endless list of questions. Is mom as healthy as she says? Is she taking her medication? Is her home safe? What happens if she falls? Even if the family understand the circumstances, older adults often need advocates to navigate the health system. Hiring professionals can help, but distance creates challenges.

Even when deterioration of health is a reason to move close to family, when a move happens, the right place may be to senior living where onsite personal care is available. When care is a key driver, particularly in situations such as dementia and memory loss, decision making often shifts from the older adult to family. Moreover, these decisions are too often made in a crisis moment with little time to prepare.

When choosing an assisted living or dementia care community, it is important to be realistic about roles and expectations. Some senior living communities welcome families, encourage visits, and look for input in mapping care plans. Others don't. Some are better run than others. Poorly managed senior living communities may not provide the peace of mind everyone seeks. And distance is an important variable. As health deteriorates, visits may feel less meaningful or more one-sided but are critical, even if may not seem that way. If a senior living community is too far away, fewer visits will happen. It's a reality.

CONCLUSION

Living with or near family is complicated, but there are a variety of options for making it work. Appreciate the importance of intergenerational interactions and friendships. If you don't live near family, there are other opportunities to develop surrogate intergenerational relationships.

With my grandparents living far away, I desired a grandparent-like relationship locally. Spurred on by a program organized by my sixth-grade teacher, I created a surrogate grandparent relationship with Melba Rowlands, a resident of a local assisted living community. In her late 70s, she was blind but otherwise healthy. Over the course of several years, we shared meals and traded gifts. My favorite was a crotched squirrel she made in her crafts class. I still have it. It was better than anything I could create.

It works both ways. If you're an older adult and don't live near family, there are ample ways to create opportunities for intergenerational interaction and friendship. In the absence of family nearby, these relationships may be just the family you need.

PART IV

THE EVOLUTION
OF PLACE

Part IV focuses on how housing is changing, particularly from a technology, health, and health care perspective. Significant advances are expected in these areas in the years ahead, and planners should carefully consider these shifts before making irreversible decisions.

CHAPTER 12

PLACE AS A HUB FOR TECHNOLOGY

The National Building Museum in Washington, DC, showcases an exhibit called *House and Home*. It includes a kaleidoscopic array of photographs, objects, models, and films to tell the story of how housing and the concept of home have evolved in America. It highlights the evolution of building materials, the impact of iconic residential homes like Fallingwater by Frank Lloyd Wright, and the expansion of financing vehicles to broaden the market of homeowners.

One of the most striking elements of the exhibit is how technology has shaped our lives within our homes. There was a time before electricity and indoor plumbing. Lighting a room required a match. There was a time before television, and when it did arrive, it was black and white, large, and incredibly heavy. There was a time when families shared one landline phone connected to a party line where neighbors could hop on the line without warning. There was no such thing as a private conversation.

Exhibits like *House and Home* evoke a sense of nostalgia and desire to go back in time to live in a different era. In that process, it's easy to overlook the significance of modern advances. Take laundry, for example. Prior to today's efficient washing machines, doing laundry was laborious and physically demanding. The process involved a prewash, a soak, a reheat of the cleaning solution, a rinse, and a dry. The entire effort could take up to 15 hours.[1]

Advances in the home have made our lives more convenient, efficient, safe, and healthy. For a variety of reasons, homes are poised to become a hub of technology.

THE FOURTH INDUSTRIAL REVOLUTION

Certain technology and academic circles have recently introduced the concept of a fourth industrial revolution.[2] The first industrial revolution occurred in the late eighteenth and early nineteenth centuries with advancements such as the steam engine that shifted the manufacturing of goods from small shops and homes to large factories and triggered a mass migration from rural areas to big cities. The second industrial revolution, also known as the technological revolution, occurred in the mid-nineteenth through the early twentieth century with breakthroughs in standardization, such as with the assembly line, and technological systems, including electrical power and telephones. The third industrial revolution is characterized by the advent of computing and the Internet and covers the period from the 1960s to 2010s.

The concept of the fourth industrial revolution, occurring today, was first described by Klaus Schwab, the executive chairman of the World Economic Forum. The fourth industrial revolution blends advances in multiple areas, including hardware, software, biology, and communication technologies to create breakthrough innovations in many areas, ranging from robotics to biotechnology to augmented reality and much more. During this period, the speed of innovation is expected to accelerate, thereby disrupting existing industries and creating new ones.

The home will likely change considerably throughout the fourth industrial revolution. Sensors will be ubiquitous, ultra-high-speed wireless networks will enable high-definition video calls, and products and services, including autonomous vehicles, will arrive on demand instantaneously. Health services, both preventative and acute, will be provided in the home and supported by robots. In other words, we're headed toward the life of the Jetsons.

SMART HOMES FROM HYPE TO REALITY

One of the odd things about technology is that it often starts with hype. Too often, unfulfilled hype. Think back to the early days of the Internet in the 1990s. Experts expected the Internet to change everything. Internet stocks skyrocketed, with little revenue and no profits following this optimism. The reality for the end user was not so pleasant. Netscape was the dominant web browser at the time and America Online (AOL) the primary email client, and one thing they both required was patience, particularly regarding dial-up access. The World Wide Web was dubbed the worldwide wait. Eventually, as we know now, the hype was more than justified.

Smart homes are in a similar position. They are beyond the hype stage but haven't arrived at a point of transformation. But it's only a matter of time.

Think of smart homes as living spaces where residents benefit from connected technology and related analytics to enhance life. Today, this involves the connection of various devices, such as appliances, lighting, and cameras, into one system that is controlled through a smartphone or voice-enabled smart speaker. It involves the ability of these devices and systems to take proactive action based on information. For example, smart refrigerators can automatically order groceries when inventory is low. Tomorrow, smart speakers will likely be able to detect a change in our voice that is suggestive of a health event, such as a stroke, and alert help.

Motivations for deploying smart home technologies can be convenience and saving money. It is convenient to control lighting, temperature, and appliances by smartphone or voice command. Sprinkler systems can be configured to conserve water. In places where water is expensive, the ability to monitor outflow can be an important cost-saving measure. Heating, ventilation, and air conditioning (HVAC) systems can do the same thing: by dividing a home into zones and setting temperatures for each zone, utility expenses can be reduced by only heating and cooling rooms that people actually use.

Another driver for adoption is safety. Video doorbells are easy to configure and allow for verbal communication with visitors without coming to the door. They can record activity to detect suspicious behaviors and coordinate with the authorities and neighbors. Networked together across homes, these systems can be effective in keeping a neighborhood safe. Smart home technology has created a wider range of home security systems from do-it-yourself packages to professional systems supported by call centers. Today it is easy and affordable to have eyes on your home.

Increasingly for older adults, smart homes offer the prospect of supporting successful aging in the home. One example are personal emergency response systems (PERS), which have been available for years. Recall the pendants advertised in low-budget television commercials with the tag line "I've fallen and I can't get up." What's different now is that with various sensor systems, either wearable devices or ones embedded in the living space, falls can be detected without hitting a button. These systems can be programmed to sense a significant change and take action. Some systems are able to detect subtle changes, such as differences in sleeping patterns, walking gait, or weight, that are suggestive of health risks. These systems create an opportunity to intervene before a significant health event occurs, such as a fall or heart attack.

Unfortunately, today's smart devices rarely work as one system. Too often, smart devices require their own app and won't interface into a broader system. But there are signs this is changing. First, in the area of voice, standards are emerging so that various smart-enabled devices can be controlled by a variety of platforms.[3] Interoperability drives adoption because consumers can more safely make investments without fear of committing to a potentially obsolete system. Second, large technology platforms are targeting homes as a key growth opportunity. As a result, these companies are investing in research and development and acquisitions to roll out innovative devices and systems. As interoperability improves and major technology companies create better devices, smart homes will move further away from hype and closer to revolutionizing the home.

ENABLING CONNECTION AND LEARNING

In-person, face-to-face communication is better than any method of communicating using technology. But communication of some sort is better than none at all. We take it as a given that we can email, text, and call at will. Understanding how our home supports communication through technology is important. Reliable high-speed broadband is no longer a nice-to-have, particularly in places such as rural areas where cell phone service is spotty.

The coronavirus pandemic was a coming-out party for video communication. Prior, most of us occasionally used one-to-one video calling features. The pandemic introduced us to capable platforms that allowed for bringing more than two people together. We learned that effective video communication needs high bandwidth, good lighting, and good acoustics, among other factors.

The ability to see someone—or be seen—can be better than just a traditional phone call. It's true in the context of personal relationships as well as professional ones. For friends and family, the ability to regularly communicate with loved ones rarely seen in person is valuable, and, as the technology improves, video communication will feel increasingly lifelike. For professional purposes, video calls can help make or reinforce a connection. Applications can simulate in-person meetings by ways such as screen sharing for presentations and breaking into smaller virtual groups. These meetings are still not the same as in-person gatherings, but they can be viable alternatives. Connected homes with the proper equipment can facilitate this experience. For older adults, the right setup enables connection with friends and family and the ability to be effective in a professional context.

A properly connected home opens up new possibilities for learning. For kids and adults alike, distance learning is now available and will be increasingly important in the future. I have a friend in Virginia whose daughter takes live video piano lessons from his brother in Maryland. Distance hasn't impeded learning, but it did require an investment in a quality camera and a high-bandwidth connection. My wife and kids are learning to play the piano without an instructor. They use an electronic piano connected to an app on a tablet that provides instruction. The app tracks which keys are hit and for how long so it can grade the accuracy of their playing. For older adults looking to be challenged intellectually, the ability to enroll in interactive online classes and other modes of learning is expanding rapidly. The art of learning, or at least where and how it occurs, is changing with smart home technology.

Over time, we may develop more of a connection to the technology itself, perhaps as a partial antidote to social isolation and loneliness. We mustn't let digital "friends" take the place of real friends. Voice-enabled interactive devices do offer an opportunity for interaction, even as limited as an automated response to "Good morning." These voice interfaces will improve as they develop the ability to differentiate voices and learn more about a person to create more customized dialogue.[4] Personalization through artificial intelligence is part of the fourth industrial revolution.

Robots will have a role in the future, too. Robots are still in the hype stage and may remain there for a while. There are some successful efforts, however, particularly in Japan, where robots are able to offer some social benefits.[5] One example is in the realm of telepresence, where a robot with a screen can be the interface for video communication with others, such as family and caregivers. For people with mobility challenges, telepresence robots can provide connectivity that would otherwise be more challenging. With greater breakthroughs in artificial intelligence, including machine learning, and as price points drop, one would expect robots to have a greater role in the lives of older adults, particularly when a robot can supplement an existing care team.

KEY IMPLICATIONS

My grandparents, part of the Greatest Generation, largely opted out of the third industrial revolution. The outlier was my dad's father, who as a scientist and an author believed the computing power and word processing capabilities of a computer outweighed the difficulties of learning to use one. My other grandfather had no interest in computers, although I think he would have benefited from them. His typed letters used Wite-Out in excess.

Opting out of technology is not a viable strategy today. Staying current with technology is a skill we must have. This doesn't mean that we need to be early adopters, but not keeping up with technology may compromise our relationships, particularly in communication with grandchildren, and health, especially as digital health tools become standard.

Investment in key infrastructure is a must. Sufficient and reliable Internet connectivity is critical, as is a smartphone and knowing how to use it. These steps are just the start, and it is a moving target.

For the vast majority of people, staying on top of technology requires help. Apple stores packed with people of all ages are proof. For my father, a visit to the Genius Bar convinced him to switch computing platforms. But as the technology ramps up in the home and invariably gets more complex, more help will be needed.

For older adults, family, friends, and professional support will likely take greater roles going forward. Adult children and older grandchildren tend to be the first line of support for older adults. As technologies become more complicated, particularly those needed for health care, more than just an answer to an occasional question may be necessary, and the consequences of a mistake may be significant, even dire. Therefore older adults need to make sure they have adequate support on a reliable basis. This may involve augmenting family and friends with professional information technology (IT) support for the applications configured in the home. Similar to how homeowners are accustomed to paying gardeners to help keep yards well maintained, installing IT infrastructure and enlisting ongoing support to make sure technology functions properly may soon become a normal duty of homeowners.

There should be an inherent bias toward simplicity and a focus on what's truly needed. Adding an incremental smart device has the possibility to crash the system unexpectedly. Complexity can also make the system unusable for some family members. This poses obvious risks in the event a skilled user is not available. The ideal situation is to meet the desired technological functionality for the home with the proper infrastructure, including speed and reliability for the underlying Internet connection, and to do so in a way that is simple and convenient for all family members and those who support it.

One of the risks in turning a home into a hub for technology is a lack of security. This risk is particularly acute when a smart home has a role in providing health care. For example, what if a resident relies on a smart speaker for emergencies, and the smart speaker is deprogrammed by a hacker? The user expects help, but the notification is never sent. This could be a life-threatening hack.

The risk of cybersecurity is real.[6] Examples abound, most notably where security cameras have been hacked. In such cases, hackers are able to view what's happening inside the home and even speak directly to frightened residents. Protection can be a challenge. Some best practices include making sure your Wi-Fi network is password protected, enabling automatic updates for apps, and using strong and unique passwords, particularly for sensitive accounts. Third-party help can be valuable. It is critical to understand the risks and impact of losing network connectivity. Having strategies for network downtime is wise, particularly for instances when functionality is mission-critical.

CONCLUSION

There is reason for skepticism about turning a home into a smart home. The benefits of convenience and safety may not justify hassles and costs. In time, however, this may turn into a minority view. As technology costs go down, the number of connected devices increases, and systems become more intuitive and reliable, more people will invest in smart homes. When they do, they must do so with an eye toward simplicity and safety.

Technology's assistance in enabling a longer and healthier life in one's preferred living environment is a big driver for technology adoption by older adults. Outfitting a home with the right technology and support may serve as an insurance policy from needing to move to a more expensive and less desirable living environment. Technologies from video communications to voice interfaces to telepresence and robots are changing rapidly, and as larger technology platforms gain more traction, more solutions will enter the marketplace.

Not only is home becoming a hub for technology—technology is also enabling the home to become the hub for health.

CHAPTER 13

PLACE AS A HUB FOR HEALTH

It's fascinating how trends can come full circle. Something is cool, goes out of fashion, and then becomes cool again. Take cargo shorts, for example. I wore them in the '80s and loved their functionality. They disappeared for a couple of decades, but now they're back. Thank goodness.

The same is true with health care. In the nineteenth century, most middle- and upper-class people were treated at home by their families when sick.[1] Surgeries were routinely performed at home. In the twentieth century, the venue for care changed as the medical profession became more sophisticated, society became more urbanized, and hospital capacity grew. Along this journey, health care costs exploded—growing at a rate higher than inflation—with policymakers now desperately trying to rein in costs. At the same time, many people would prefer to not go to the hospital. Fear of getting sick is one reason and of particular concern during a pandemic. This points to a return to the past: using the home as a hub for health and health care.[2]

Technology and health care services in the community are making the shift back to home possible. Some insurers and health providers offer 24-7 telehealth support, remote patient monitoring, and home health equipment. Health care and care services, such as personal care and companionship, private duty nursing care, and home health care,

are available in many communities. People with complicated, acute health conditions can now be taken care of at home.

The implication is that home is taking on an increasingly significant role. The right home increases the odds of staying healthy, and when health fades, it can be a place where health care services can be delivered efficiently and cost effectively. The wrong place introduces health risks and raises the odds of needing to move to receive care.

PLACE AS AN ENABLER OF WELLNESS

Our built environments have the potential to improve our wellness. We spend about 90% of our time indoors, yet historically there hasn't been much of a focus on how our indoor environment affects us.[3] There is a movement to change this shortcoming.

One approach is to incorporate nature in the built environment. Architects call this biophilic design. The idea of accessing nature in our physical environments is not new. What's changed is that as cities and suburbs have expanded, nature has been crowded out. Humans were not designed to live in a concrete jungle; our bodies respond positively to nature.

Biophilic design includes direct and indirect experiences with nature. Direct experiences include natural light, quality air, water as a soothing agent, plants, and access to natural landscapes. Indirect experiences of nature include images of nature, the use of natural materials, and the incorporation of natural colors. These elements can be incorporated within a built environment as well as broadly within a metropolitan area. Singapore, for example, stands out with its system of nature preserves, parks and connectors, and tree-lined streets that promote the return of wildlife and reduce the heat island effect. The heat island effect occurs particularly in urban areas, where the concentration of development, including buildings and concrete, contributes to higher heat values.

Research points to the positive impact of biophilic elements in living environments. Mental health improves when urban noise is substituted with nature sounds. Surgery patients use significantly less pain medicine when exposed to aromatherapy, and plants in interior environments reduce stress and increase pain tolerance.[4]

Real estate developers are incorporating wellness into their design. Two industry certifications—the WELL Building Standard (WELL) created by Delos and administered by the International WELL Building Institute and Fitwel launched by the Centers for Disease Control and Prevention and the General Services Administration and operated by the nonprofit Center for Active Design—provide an ability to validate that built environments have incorporated and maintain elements integral for wellness. In a sense, these bodies are providing a certification akin to Leadership in Energy and Environmental Design (LEED), the widely adopted green building certification for real estate. These certification entities include biophilia in their evaluation and take additional steps to promote health. They measure, certify, and monitor features that affect human health and well-being through air, light, water, nourishment, fitness, comfort, and mind.

Developing or remodeling a single-family house to the WELL or Fitwel standard may be more than is necessary and could be cost prohibitive. Several steps can be taken to make a physical environment healthier, however. One can invest in air filtration systems, particularly if respiratory health is a concern. Add indoor plants. Consider window treatments that allow for maximum light. Use natural materials. Add a water filter or water cooler in a convenient location to encourage water consumption. There's a long list of potential interventions to consider.

Pay particular attention to the bedroom. As discussed in chapter 1, sleep has a significant impact on our bodies and minds. Consider the lighting and temperature that work best for you. Evaluate the suitability of your mattress. If sleep is a challenge, consider modifications and experiments to see if a change might be beneficial. Improvements in this area can provide a particularly high return on wellness.

Don't forget about outdoor space. It is easier to incorporate nature in single-family homes than in apartments or condos, but opportunities exist to include nature in virtually any environment. Creating a private outdoor place, even on a balcony, can provide opportunities to commune with nature. Make spaces welcoming. Include potted plants wherever possible. If parks are close by, organize your daily or weekly routine to visit them.

As wellness design proliferates, there will be more certified housing options, including apartment buildings, condominiums, and senior living communities. National homebuilders are incorporating healthy elements in new developments. There are many options to consider if enhancing well-being through the physical environment is a priority.

PLACE AS A HUB FOR CARE AND HEALTH CARE SERVICES

We are reaching a point where the range of care and health care services a person can receive at home is nearly limitless. Care services focus on activities of daily living (ADLs), such as bathing and dressing, and instrumental activities of daily living (IADLs), such as shopping, cooking, and managing medications. Health care services are those that could be provided in a hospital or medical setting, such as physician care, nursing care, and therapy services.

Care in the home, as opposed to in a long-term care setting, is nothing new. What is new is the wide range of offerings for care. Private duty home care is a popular option with providers that are increasingly using technology to provide better and more efficient care. Care can be expensive, generally ranging from $15 to $20 per hour and potentially exceeding $4,000 per month if used heavily.[5] A more affordable option is to utilize adult daycare supplemented by support from family and other caregivers. Adult daycare provides a range of care services, including socialization and ADL support, from a centralized location. It is less expensive than private duty home care, averaging $1,625 per month.[6]

Think back to Bob in chapter 2. With his plan to remain in his house, Bob will likely eventually need care at his house. Recall that about 70% of people 65 and older will need long-term care at some point in their lifetime.[7] It will be important that he selects a quality provider that he can afford. Coordinating this care can be complicated and may require his family's oversight.

Health care services are increasingly oriented toward home. For example, MedStar Health is a not-for-profit health system in the Mid-Atlantic that provides house calls for older adults.[8] The MedStar House Call Program is nationally recognized for quality and outcomes of care and provides a number of services that otherwise would be provided in a hospital. This includes the ability to get vital signs, draw blood, and take basic tests, including x-rays in some cases. They deploy a team-based approach that includes physicians and physician assistants, nurse practitioners, case managers, and social workers to all work together for the good of the patient. The goal of the program is to allow people to stay in their homes, a situation preferable for the people it serves and less expensive than repeated hospital visits.

The proliferation of telehealth has accelerated the availability of health care services in the home. In response to the coronavirus pandemic, telehealth regulations have loosened to provide reimbursement for physicians wherever a patient is located. Telehealth services include virtual emergency room visits, nursing visits, therapy services, and more. Telehealth has also made it easier for multiple health care professionals to coordinate and communicate with patients and their families. These advances serve people in single-family houses and apartments as well as residents in senior living who couple telehealth services within in-person care teams.

As care and health care shifts to the home, you and your support network must be able to handle what's involved. For example, with technology like telehealth, do you have the space, infrastructure, and support to be able to manage what's required? This may mean creating a physical space for health care equipment and ensuring that Internet and cellular connections are fast and reliable. Be realistic about what is needed. You may need help beyond what a health care provider offers.

IMPORTANCE OF FLEXIBILITY AND USABILITY

One of the key implications of utilizing home as a hub for health is the need to design for flexibility. It is best to think of our homes in the context of our current as well as our future health. This means that a home need not be designed for every health contingency, nor must young homebuyers consider how their home could support them in their 90s. However, understanding the flexibility of a home is an important consideration for older adults. Place—from region to metropolitan area to neighborhood to the built environment—needs to be considered through the lens of health. A fail point at any level may be enough to force someone into a housing situation that they don't wish but can't avoid.

Important areas are the accessibility and safety of our physical dwelling. Can your home integrate universal design elements, such as a stair-free environment, bathroom with low-clearance showers, and wide entryways, if and when such elements are needed? This is a matter of convenience and safety. A home that has unavoidable fall risks may simply be the wrong place at a certain age and stage.

A former neighbor of mine in her 70s was planning to stay in her single-family house but was ultimately unable to make it work. She modified her home, including relocating her bedroom to the first floor and adding universal design elements to her bathroom, but the ultimate deciding factor was that her driveway was too steep. It became too difficult for her to navigate, particularly in snow. It was hard for care providers to reliably come to her. Because her single-family house could not enable her continued independence and autonomy, she moved to senior living earlier than envisioned.

Usability is significant. For example, if working from home is important, does your space accommodate such a use? Given the prevalence of video calls, a workspace with a professional background may be important. Consider spaces for exercise. Without spaces to stretch and be active, you are likely to be sedentary more than is recommended. If space is not usable in the ways you wish, a change may be necessary.

Consider the environment around your physical dwelling from the standpoint of health. Walking regularly is a healthy habit but unlikely to happen if your neighborhood is unsafe. Hilly neighborhoods can cut both ways. For some, living in a hilly location is a deterrent to walking. For others, such as Sufferfesters, hills represent a training opportunity.

When thinking about home as a hub for health, it may be important to consider living spaces for family or a caregiver. Is there a spare bedroom for someone who could help with caregiving should it become necessary? Do you have space for the addition of a bedroom or an accessible dwelling unit for such a purpose? Mapping out possible contingencies is important for any robust plan.

PREPARING FOR THE NEXT PANDEMIC

Unfortunately, COVID-19 will likely not be the last pandemic. Part of the silver lining of the crisis is that it has alerted many to the importance of preparation for calamitous events. Regrettably, however, there are no easy solutions.

The coronavirus pandemic highlighted the risks of density. Density can spread and accelerate infectious diseases. Dense places without sufficient outdoor space can make a stressful environment worse. Urban living typically involves a trade-off of less personal space for more shared space and amenities, like restaurants, coffee shops, and parks. The challenge during a pandemic is that shared spaces are closed off and life is limited to small personal spaces. The limitations can be traumatic; for people particularly concerned about this risk, urban living may be not be the right place.

Density in physical dwellings presents similar risks. Whether located in urban settings or not, apartments and senior living pose greater risks than single-family housing simply because the dynamic of many people living close together presents increased chance of health problems.

Apartments can be dangerous during pandemics for a host of reasons. The range of services and staffing models is limited. There is neither a capability for infection control nor the manpower to oversee such a process. Apartments rely on an honor system that people do the right thing. If you are sick, self-quarantine. Particularly in pandemics with asymptotic carriers and where testing is limited, residents of apartments may fear that any neighbor is a carrier. This concern makes even simple things, like sharing an elevator with a stranger, stressful. Older adults might feel as though they need to shelter in place even if that is not required in the area they live.

This was the experience of an older couple that moved from a single-family house into an urban high-rise apartment just before the COVID-19 pandemic. They were excited for their new chapter in life, but with the pandemic, the reality of their day-to-day lived experience was much different than their expectations. Fear of contracting the disease from asymptomatic residents who were often younger and not as concerned about the health risks pinned them in their small apartment. They were scared to use the elevator. They terminated their lease and relocated. Although the media has characterized senior living as a dangerous environment during the pandemic, they felt that living in a dense apartment could be equally troublesome.

Managing a health crisis in senior living is complicated. Senior living organizations have a range of capabilities, including infection control, and staff to reliably deliver services. These are assets. But senior living must rigorously protect all its residents, which may lead to facility-wide quarantine and a reduction or elimination of visitors, including family members. Being cut off from family, particularly during end-of-life situations, can be a nightmare. The fear of this outcome alone may dissuade people from senior living.

My Aunt Dawn and Uncle Rick, mentioned in chapter 9, fared well living in senior living during the pandemic. They lived in a cottage and had meals delivered to them. They took walks and socially distanced with neighbors. Having access to care and nursing professionals close by, should they need it, was reassuring. The pandemic reaffirmed the wisdom of their move to senior living.

Living in a single-family house during a pandemic has its own challenges. There may be less risk of catching an infectious disease than in a densely populated living environment. But isolation from others for an extended period of time creates social isolation and raises the risk of loneliness and depression. Products and services, including meals, can be delivered, but it requires effort and additional expense. If a health event occurs, there is no infrastructure to support you. Avoiding a trip to the ER if possible is advisable in general, but particularly during a pandemic. In the absence of support and if there is a pressing health concern present, however, a call for help may be the best option.

Intergenerational living is complicated during a pandemic. The support structure of family can be essential, particularly during times of elevated risk and anxiety. Yet family members can be carriers of disease and catalysts for getting infected. Intergenerational living was responsible for many deaths during the COVID-19 crisis.

Unfortunately, there is no silver bullet for handling pandemics. Each option has significant trade-offs. During the COVID-19 pandemic, I have had friends who expeditiously moved loved ones out of senior living and into their homes despite the daily care responsibilities, friends who opted to stay in senior living and were comfortable with their choice, and friends who hunkered down in single-family houses and managed, particularly with the help of attentive neighbors. It is important to assess the pros and cons of each option so that you are not surprised when the unexpected occurs. Having a contingency plan is valuable regardless of the setting.

Abetted by the COVID-19 crisis, health will be more top of mind for real estate developers, policymakers, and health officials. Over time, urban environments will be retooled with consideration for how to handle pandemics. A likely result will be the adoption of more public spaces, such as parks wider sidewalks, where possible. Apartment and condo buildings will be encouraged to adopt designs that create access to fresh and higher-quality air, as well as accessible dwelling units, elevators, and amenity spaces with a limited need to use their hands. More buildings of all types will adopt health as a consideration within their environments, whether adhering to the WELL or Fitwel standards or incorporating bits and pieces as they deem appropriate.

Senior living may undergo the most radical change. Images and stories of failing nursing homes during the coronavirus crisis will not easily be forgotten, nor should they be. Infection controls will be stronger. Senior living teamed with local health officials and health systems will create new operational flows to better coordinate during pandemics. Communities will look to create larger personal spaces so that when lockdowns do occur, residents have more space. Activities and other means of socialization will have a virtual component available. Technology will be incorporated to deliver care and health care with less reliance on human-to-human contact. These communities will not be unprepared in the future.

CONCLUSION

Our homes are central to our health. They can be designed to keep us healthy and create flexibility to serve our needs as health changes. They need to be resilient, too. Pandemics and natural disasters are not hypothetical risks. With climate change and geopolitical threats, black swan events may occur more regularly. We are best not to be caught off guard.

Technology and policy are driving some of these changes. Health care will be increasingly provided in the home virtually with on-demand services. Incentives are aligning to the point where living in lower-care and lower-cost settings will be feasible and advantageous for consumers and health care payors.

The best of all worlds is to create a home environment that keeps us healthy, helps us recover from health events, and enables effective management of chronic diseases. It requires a thoughtful approach to designing and managing our physical environment. Choosing home—the right home at a given time and stage—requires more careful planning than ever before.

PART V

TAKING ACTION

Part V prompts the reader to take specific action by either making the most of their current living situation or launching a process to select, move to, and settle into a new place.

CHAPTER 14

MAKING THE MOST OF YOUR CURRENT PLACE

Think back to your self-evaluation in chapter 2. You were prompted to reflect on areas in your life that drive overall well-being, including purpose, social connection, physical well-being, financial well-being, and place. Where are the gaps between where you are and where you would like to be?

It is important to recognize that well-being can be improved without moving from one's current home. Despite the significant influence of place on our well-being, there are other important variables that should not be overlooked. Besides, moving can be one of the hardest types of change, and change tends to get much more difficult as we age.

Sometimes, moving is not feasible, even when it would be the best path. Maybe the emotional connection to your current place is too great to sever. Perhaps you are not psychologically ready for a change, such as shortly after losing a spouse. Maybe it is not financially possible because the current real estate market is not favorable for sellers.

Whether staying where you are is the best choice or moving is not a viable option, the opportunity becomes how to make the most of one's current living situation.

AREAS OF OPPORTUNITY
BEYOND PLACE

There are ways to enhance purpose without changing place. If you work, it could be looking for opportunities for growth and making an increased impact in your current role or transitioning to a job within your organization that's a better fit for your current life, maybe part-time. This could be finding a new job suited for your current interests or pursuing an encore career that gives back. It could be volunteering in your community by being a resource to your neighbors and family or getting more involved in a civic organization or place of worship. Maybe it is taking up a cause you feel passionate about, like combating climate change or fighting for social justice. You could help a friend who is going through a hard time, or you may wish carve out time to be with family. Sitting down and thinking through opportunities for greater purpose before making significant changes in place could be time well spent.

There are ways to create strong social connections without moving elsewhere. You can make an effort to reconnect with old friends in the area or welcome new neighbors with the prospect of creating new friendships. You can start a new tradition in the neighborhood that brings people together, such as a book club or neighborhood volunteering organization. Consider taking up a cause in your area and rallying friends to join you so that you can spend time on something you care about with people you value. You can be more intentional about connecting with good friends who live elsewhere and consider visiting each other more often.

Physical well-being can be boosted without necessarily a change of scene. Wearables, such as smartwatches, are becoming more capable, affordable, and mainstream. These devices track and motivate users toward greater levels of activity. Buying a wearable device and joining an online community could help you become more active. Smartphone apps can help you monitor and improve eating habits and sleeping patterns. Joining a local gym or investing in a home gym could be a valuable step. Home gyms are getting increasingly sophisticated and are considerably safer during pandemics. Becoming more physically active can be as simple as finding a walking or bicycling buddy to get with on a regular basis.

Financial well-being is an important lever that can be improved without moving. There are ways to increase income or cut costs to prepare for the years ahead. As with any financial plan, it's important to have realistic expectations. Working for a long time in your career or current job may not mesh with the realities of the marketplace. You may have to be open to part-time work or entrepreneurial ventures, which often do not provide the same level of consistent income streams. Plus, investment professionals generally recommend investment portfolios be more conservative as people age, limiting potential investment returns. You may need to be opportunistic to create additional streams of income, such as with home sharing. Managing expenses is also important. But cost cutting has its limits before it starts to affect quality of life. Some older adults let the fear of running out of money influence their investment in health. Purchasing lower-quality produce or avoiding preventative trips to the doctor may save money in the short term, but these decisions have more significant long-term costs. It's best to watch costs and identify areas of opportunity. Utilizing one of the increasingly prevalent online financial tools, seeking assistance from friends or family, or hiring professional advisors can be helpful tools for managing your finances.

While place matters, it may not be the primary culprit holding you back from a better life. Making little bets, whether it be in the areas of purpose, social connection, physical well-being, or financial well-being may surprise you with their impact. Some bets cut across multiple dimensions, like how joining a walking group helps with physical activity and social connection. Brainstorming ideas with others may be fruitful. You can try out ideas with nearby friends or with friends elsewhere. Find out which ideas work and why.

AREAS OF OPPORTUNITY
WITHIN PLACE

Even if you are not moving to a new place, there are opportunities to make your current place better. Some options may require meaningful financial investment, but plenty don't.

A good place to start is decluttering and finding joy in it. The queen of organizing is Marie Kondo, author of *The Life-Changing Magic of Tidying Up*.[1] Kondo suggests focusing on whether an item brings joy. If not, you should feel comfortable discarding it without guilt. If it does bring joy, find a place for it. She recommends tackling clutter by category rather than by room. For example, rather than sort books in your bedroom, pool all of your books and determine which to keep. There are countless techniques to declutter; what's important is that you find an approach and a frequency that works for you.

Decluttering can be overwhelming and can often benefit from the input of others. Friends can help friends. Family can step in. My wife is a go-to resource in her family. She's been called on countless times to be an objective voice on what to keep and what to discard. If she helps someone who wears similar size clothes, she may walk away with some parting gifts. One person's trash can be another's treasure. There are also professionals who can help. Don't think that you must do it alone.

Decluttering has some clear benefits. For me, the purging process is freeing. Once I get into it, there's a satisfaction in identifying possessions that would be best to find a new owner. The best stuff can go to consignment shops, and decent stuff can go to a thrift store. The process allows me to better appreciate my possessions. Decluttering helps prepare for a change in place in the future. It can lower the psychological hurdle of a move as well as help understand how much stuff you may need at your current stage in life.

Another opportunity is to change the look and function of spaces. This can be as simple as rearranging furniture. During one of her visits, my sister-in-law resituated our kitchen table. It changed the whole feel for the better, and I was unaware that such a change was possible. Similar changes may be available to you. Consider the impact of adding a fresh coat of paint to a room. It can create a new look. There are lots of small changes that can reinvigorate a space and your interest in using it. Plus, these are low-risk changes: if you don't like it, you can easily switch back.

Particularly for those living in single-family houses where children were raised, it can be helpful to revisit the best purpose of each room. Sometimes, children's rooms can sit idly for years as a tribute to them. Some friends have fallen into this trap. One family's daughter left for college more than 20 years ago and now lives overseas, yet her room sits almost unchanged. Space for that extra office, guest room, or den may already exist, but it may require emotionally moving on from prior uses.

Friends of mine in their 70s gave strong consideration to moving from their home of more than 30 years. The couple loved their house, but it had lost some of its charm and took a lot of effort to maintain. They explored other options in their area but found nothing that excited them. They decided to remodel their house. With an update of the kitchen, rearranging of several walls, and a new décor, it was as if they were in a new home. Part of their success was in reimagining their house, which allowed them to make changes they would not have made had their children still been around. Some of their changes included universal design aspects, but it was mostly about aesthetics and usability.

If extra space is available in an existing home, it can be utilized to accommodate others. As we explored in chapter 10, an existing home with extra space can be used to house a roommate for social benefits, income, or both. Existing space can also be for used for social purposes. Host a book club. Start a porch party. Be a destination for friends after a faith service. One of the benefits of hosting others is that ideas to improve your space naturally emerge. Good friends may be particularly candid. They may provide the prompting necessary to convert an old kids' room to a space of greater utility.

Renovation, no matter the scale, is a key consideration for many homeowners. Spaces can be transformed on the basis of the desired uses and look of today. For those who wish to age in their homes over the long haul and have homes where such a desire is possible, a renovation can be critical to incorporate common universal design elements and technology infrastructure. Technology and the intersection of health and health care, the subjects of chapters 12 and 13, should be carefully considered. There is a lot that can be done, depending on needs and budget.

Adding an accessible dwelling unit should be considered if there is available land and zoning permits such a use. ADUs, depending on the jurisdiction, can be an opportunity for incremental rental revenue while still offering private space to you and renters. ADUs offer the optionality as a potential dwelling for you or your loved ones. One of the advantages of an ADU is that it can be designed in an age-friendly manner, including considerations for technology and mobility, more easily than within an existing house. It's possible to create a space that is attractive and flexible for a variety of uses.

Renters, either for apartments or houses, can also consider renovation possibilities. Apartment owners value long-term, responsible tenants. If an apartment is modified to enhance a kitchen or bathroom, owners may be willing to absorb the cost in exchange for a longer lease commitment. Circumstances can be similar in the case of single-family rental homes. If the owner sees value in a modification that could lead to higher rent from future tenants, they may not require an additional commitment. The key is to have a conversation with the owner or primary decision maker to see what's possible. You may have more luck with private owners than with institutional groups that may be bound by companywide policies.

Renovation can play a role for those living in senior living environments as well. Some communities allow you to customize your unit before moving in. If you have ideas for improving your living space, share them with management. Moreover, senior living communities have dollars reserved in their capital budgets for renovations and improvements to amenity spaces. If it's important to you, be vocal and try to influence the allocation of monies. For example, if a fitness area needs updating and exercising is important to you, get involved and connect with other residents to voice this concern to ownership. You will be more persuasive if the desired changes align with the desires of future residents. Ownership groups make capital investments to improve the lives of existing residents but are generally more mindful of future residents in order to keep their communities competitive. Investing in improvements that both appeal to current and future residents and strengthen a community for its owners is a win-win-win.

One area that can get overlooked is finding ways to reduce the ongoing costs of a home. Renovating a home can create opportunities for investment that create long-term advantages and cost savings. Examples for savings can include adding solar panels, fuel-efficient water heaters, water-efficient sprinkler systems, insulation, and more. When taking a long view of the total cost of ownership of your home, these investments can represent a high return on investment. It may attract additional interest from potential homebuyers and perhaps a higher purchase price.

As one example, I have friends who live on the East Coast in a stately home built in the 1890s. It has charm not often found in modern homes. But it lacks the energy efficiency that most modern homes have. After their first winter living in the house, they were overwhelmed by the energy costs, which averaged thousands of dollars per month. The house was too leaky, and it was impossible to plug all of the holes without a significant rebuild. They were concerned that potential buyers would be scared off by the energy costs. They decided to invest in a geothermal energy system, which required digging about 100 feet into their yard to create a loop system that was far more efficient year-round. It was a substantial financial outlay but provided a return on investment within several years and protects their investment in their home.

Technology has an important role in maintaining health within the home. Technology to support successful aging is a rapidly changing field, with innovations introduced regularly. These advances are affecting those with moderate as well as significant health issues. For example, investing in a remote patient monitoring kit that includes a blood pressure monitor, pulse oximeter, cellular-enabled digital tablet, and a digital scale can help those with congestive heart failure stay at home.[2] Relatively small investments in technology can have a high impact on health and increase the odds of staying in your home.

When it comes to renovation, there's wisdom in not trying to account for every possibility or future outcome. For example, if the idea is to age-proof your home, it may be best to focus on the biggies—safety and usability of your bathroom, for example—and tackle other projects on an as-needed basis. If you go through the trouble and expense of making an environment wheelchair-friendly and you don't have a need, you may end up preparing for a scenario that does not come to pass. The same strategy can hold for technology adoption, too. Waiting to invest in a technology solution until you need it may result in a lower cost and more reliable product than if you were an early adopter.

SPECIAL CONSIDERATIONS FOR
CLOSE FRIENDS AND FAMILY, INCLUDING
ADULT CHILDREN

It is human nature to have blind spots. It seems that as we age these blind spots expand, particularly in how we see ourselves versus our reality. People often don't accurately perceive changes in health and the risks these changes cause. Often it seems that friends and family are more likely to observe changes and their implications than the loved one.

This gap between perception and reality can create risks and tensions when considering living situations. A common and significant challenge is when a parent or loved one lives in an environment that is no longer appropriate, yet they are unwilling to change. In these scenarios, an existing home can represent significant hazards, such as fall risks, social isolation, and loneliness. A friend or family member may try to intervene, but the loved one may stonewall their efforts because risks aren't seen or there is no interest in making a change. Denial of reality can be a challenge for all involved.

It is important to respect the living choices of loved ones, particularly when they don't pose risks to those around them. Forcing someone out of their home is a challenging path. It can create bitterness and animosity that can negatively affect relationships. In cases where loved ones are of sound mind, a friend or family member is wise to make recommendations and encourage the consideration of other options but go no further.

When there is a mismatch between a loved one's current home and needs and change is unlikely, it is best to focus on how to make the best of the current situation and create a contingency plan for when circumstances change. A friend or family member can brainstorm ways to improve the current living situation, such as through changes in lifestyle habits or modifications to the physical environment, and be a resource to help implement changes. At the same time, it can be valuable to create a series of "What if?" scenarios.

There is nothing like a health event, such as a fall, to narrow the gap between perception and reality and help clarify the risks of a particular environment. Even a health event to a friend or family member in similar circumstances can alert a loved one to risks. Even if the decision remains to stay in the same place, a health event can spur changes to the current environment as well as efforts toward contingency planning for the future.

For people who have dementia, the path forward is different. The pace of memory loss varies, which can make planning difficult. Mild cognitive decline may not pose a meaningful threat within a current living environment. In situations where the disease progresses rapidly or a loved one has significant memory loss, however, friends or family are best to initiate a change and may need to do so without the consent of the loved one. The risks of living in the wrong environment affect not just a loved one but those living nearby. For example, in an apartment setting, a fire mistakenly started by someone with dementia could become deadly for others in the building.

Making changes for people with dementia is challenging for many reasons, not the least of which is the emotional difficulty of making a change when a loved one has diminished significantly. There can be so much grief in the process of making a change, particularly if it involves moving a loved one into dementia care, that it can feel like an emotional loss of a person without the physical loss.

It is best for loved ones to craft their own plan as they age. Friends and family can help encourage loved ones to plan for future health events. But, for a variety of reasons, such planning may not happen, and friends and family are left in the unenviable position of helping or leading the process for a loved one. This is made particularly challenging when a loved one's preferences diverge from what is best environment for them.

A CHECKLIST FOR NEXT STEPS

If you plan to stay in your current home, use the checklist below to help consider and monitor all the factors:

- ☐ Verify that you and your partner, if applicable, feel comfortable in your home. If not, identify areas of concern, and break them out by those that involve a modification of your home and those that do not. Prioritize concerns, taking note of what involves significant time, energy, and resources and what does not.

- ☐ Seek feedback on your concerns with friends and family and professionals, wherever appropriate. Those who know and care for you may offer a valuable perspective. Physicians, lawyers, and financial planners bring expertise in their domain plus experience that may be helpful. They may point out areas of concern that you don't see. While considering the input of others is important, be mindful that you are ultimately responsible for your choices and know best how to satisfy your needs and desires. Don't make your decisions based on the desires of others, or else you may find yourself in a suboptimal situation.

- ☐ Track down additional resources, including professional help wherever appropriate, in key areas of concern. Better understand what can be done, if anything, to address key areas. Put together a budget of time and resources to address concerns.

☐ Take action wherever appropriate and by priority. If the time is right to go through a bathroom renovation, then move ahead. If smaller changes are not a high priority but require little effort, consider making those changes sooner rather than later.

☐ Make a contingency plan. Think about how things may change and what can be done in your current environment to accommodate these changes and at what cost. Gain a realistic sense of the conditions under which your current environment is appropriate. Recognize that not all of these conditions apply to your housing. For example, changes in tax and regulatory policy at the federal, state, or municipal level may trigger a desire for change. Simply put, understand that your metropolitan area or neighborhood may trend in a direction that makes it a less desirable place to live.

☐ Get organized around your desires concerning end-of-life scenarios. Make sure your will, trust, power of attorney, health care power of attorney, health care directives, Health Insurance Portability and Accountability Act (HIPAA) release, and other related documents are up to date and reflect your intentions. Your advanced care directive should include some direction about your living preferences.

For those looking after a loved one, there are some other factors to include:

☐ Understand and document a loved one's preference for place now and in the future. It can be valuable to have these desires in writing, even if only in email. It is best to understand not only the what and where, but the why as well. Recognize that some of these scenarios may require demands of you, whether they be financial, emotional, or with your time.

☐ Understand the suitability of the current situation from your perspective. Think through the needs of your loved one, and come to your own conclusion about the appropriateness of the current situation. If possible, seek input from friends of your loved one and their physicians, particularly if there are health care concerns.

☐ Make a contingency plan. Independently of conversations with your loved ones, think through likely scenarios as conditions change. Create a file with notes and thoughts. The more you have prepared for potential outcomes, the easier and quicker you will be able to react if and when circumstances change.

☐ Be encouraging and supportive of your loved one. People don't like to think about death or the deterioration of health. The uncertainty of certain outcomes creates anxiety. Err on the side of compassion and tenderness in your communications.

☐ Communicate regularly and be available. Particularly when loved ones live far away, it is easy to get caught up in the busyness of life. As cliche as it may sound, make time for mom and dad. Regular communication will help in picking up on changes in perspectives and behavior. It will also allow for casual and fun conversations, not just those focused on health needs or planning. Be available when a loved one reaches out. Sometimes the most seemingly innocuous call or voice mail may belie an urgent and important need. It's hard for parents to be viewed as burdens to their adult children, so they may mask needs and risks. It's important to uncover them in a timely manner.

☐ Consider adding technology tools. Look into ways technology can be helpful in communicating with a loved one as well as provide insights into their health. For example, video calls may tell you more about a person's condition than a phone call. There are other technologies, such as sensors, that can be used to help monitor one's health or provide infrastructure for a quick response in the event of an emergency. By collaborating with loved ones and understanding their preferences, a modest investment in technology can make home a suitable solution for a longer period of time. If technology becomes a lynchpin in helping a loved one stay in their current dwelling, help them figure out the best options and also the best way to support these technologies. You are likely to be tier one support, so finding a solution that meets your needs is an important consideration.

CONCLUSION

One of the best parts of staying in one's home is that it limits the risks of making a poor decision. Imagine moving with the expectation that changing locations would dramatically improve life, only to find that a change didn't improve anything. In fact, it may make life worse. In such a situation, maybe the wrong lever was pulled. Improvement could have been made by investing in greater purpose, better social connection, or being more physically active.

The reality is that lifestyle changes are often too difficult to make in our current setting. We get set in our ways. Mixing things up by changing places can be just what's needed to trigger other, broader changes. Alternative options need to be considered when our health is at risk. Regardless of the particulars, there are conditions for which a change in place is the wrong move and others where a change in place is the right move.

CHAPTER 15

SELECTING A NEW PLACE

The circumstances that lead to a change of place vary. In general, they come in two forms: pull and push.[1] Pull factors are situations where the allure of an environment compels someone to move. Push factors are situations where one's home is no longer the best place and a move elsewhere is a prudent decision.

Chapter 2 highlighted people motivated to move to a better place. Mike and Lisa left Buffalo for Dallas to start a new chapter as empty nesters and move into a home and life more appropriate for them. This change provided greater purpose, stronger social connection, and increased opportunities to be active. Krishna and Mamta moved to an intergenerational community closer to good friends and community to enjoy a deeper social connection. Robert and Lucinda relocated from a single-family house in the suburbs of New Jersey to be a part of their daughter's family's life and to live in a growing metropolitan area. In all of these examples, pull was the primary driver for the move.

Gail's story is a mix of pull and push. She moves to a retirement community to satisfy her craving for social connection with more people like her and desire to be active and eat healthily. She loves her house and will miss its memories but recognizes that she does not have a viable plan for care as she ages. It is a wise move but one with mixed emotions.

CALIBRATING THE RISKS OF MOVING

Moving is a hassle, expensive, and stressful. The biggest hurdle, particularly for older adults, is that of risk: it's hard to undo, despite what we may think. Consider selling a large home, downsizing, and moving into a small home. For many, particularly those who have lived in a large home for years, if not decades, it is a challenging process logistically, physically, emotionally, psychologically, and more. To undertake that level of effort only to find that your new place is not what you expected can be deflating at best and prompt feeling despondent at worst.

The initial instinct may be to reverse your decision. Why can't I go back to the way things used to be? It's often not that simple. The prior house has been sold, and possessions have been jettisoned. Transaction and transition costs add up. It may not be financially feasible. But more than this, your prior life, in a sense, has ended. The chapter has closed. A poor decision may require another change, but not one that re-creates your original situation and circumstance.

My friend Doug and his wife experienced the consequences of making a poor decision about place. They were empty nesters living in suburban Austin. Their house was larger than they needed and required more maintenance than they desired. Doug's job was downtown, and the commute irritated him. He and his wife spent a lot of time in the city and enjoyed its restaurants, music venues, and gathering places.

They decided to move to the city. They sold their house, ridded themselves of possessions, and moved into a condo apartment in a high-rise building. At first, they loved it. Doug walked to work. They ate out and listened to live music often. They enjoyed the lifestyle of urban living.

In time, reservations about their decision emerged. They missed their friends in the suburbs. They found it hard to meet new friends in their new environment. Meaningful social connection was elusive. They longed for more space. Their guest room couldn't hold their family during the holidays. Doug's wife missed her garden.

After several years, they decided to move back to the suburbs. Their old house was not available, and it was too big. Finding a house the size and location they preferred took months and was pricey. It was an expensive decision, as they absorbed transaction fees on two homes, paid a premium for their new house, and increased their annual real estate tax bill. They even had to purchase new furniture because they jettisoned most of their furniture when they downsized. They were fortunate to be able to move back to the prior area, but it was not without stress and expense.

WHERE TO GO: THE IMPORTANCE OF DILIGENCE

Picking a new place to live is fraught with uncertainty. A move of any type requires openness to risk. As no move is seamless, it's helpful to have the mindset of adventure, not disaster. Moving can present one hurdle after another without warning.

One of the first steps is to narrow your decision tree. For some, this is not challenging. They know where they want to be. There's no sense in overanalyzing the situation. Just do it.

For most of us, moving is not simple when it involves big, life-changing decisions. These decisions are made more complicated when others are involved, whether it be a spouse, a partner, or a friend or family member that may be affected by our decision.

Following a process can be helpful. One approach is to start wide and get narrow. Determine what region and metropolitan area you wish to live in. Look back to chapter 4. Use the framework and tools to get smart on options, including the various pros and cons of each potential area. Then, think about elements of neighborhood and community, the subject of chapter 5. Once there is clarity on these variables, then finding the right dwelling takes on greater priority.

Consider the importance of time. Perhaps you are certain of where you want to go, but the timing is not right. Be mindful that the best decision is not just choosing the best place for you, but the best place for you at the right time. This can mean an acceleration or delay of your plans depending on the circumstances.

Keep in mind that there is no one universal process that works for everyone. It is important to weigh your decision carefully, however, recognizing its impact on your life and future and the risks and downsides of getting it wrong. Sometimes, breaking your decision into a series of smaller bets can be a wise way to go.

USE DESIGN THINKING TO FIND YOUR PLACE

As discussed in chapter 2, design thinking is a method of taking small bets based on a series of hypotheses and observing how they work in real life. Learn, make changes, and iterate to find a better solution. Design thinking is important for finding place because it can be a way of testing options before making a commitment. When the decisions are big and potentially irreversible, design thinking can be key in mitigating risk.

Design thinking could have helped Doug and his wife in their decision to move to the city. Going in, they had a number of hypotheses. They were assuming that they would enjoy the urban lifestyle (true), Doug would have an easier commute (true), they could make friends (false), and they would be satisfied with their small space in a high-rise apartment (false). These untrue hypotheses outweighed the true ones and triggered another change in place.

Doug and his wife could have spent more energy testing their hypotheses before moving. They were confident that they would enjoy the entertainment of the city, and Doug's work was objectively much closer. Hypotheses about the urban lifestyle and easier commute were not risky.

The uncertainty was with their ability to create community and live in a small urban apartment. They could have reached out to friends and acquaintances who relocated from the suburbs to the city to understand in detail how satisfied they were with the move and what they learned in the process. They could have researched the culture of some of the apartment condominium buildings and nearby areas to get a feel for whether the people who lived there were their type. It may have helped them understand how confident or concerned they should be about creating social connection. There were multiple ways that they could have tested whether living in a small apartment would work for them. They could have rented an apartment for a weekend or a month to get a feel for fit and size. A more helpful experiment would have been to rent an apartment for a year and rent out their house at the same time. This would have given them a more complete taste of urban life while still retaining the option to move back to their home.

Design thinking is useful because it tests whether what we think is true is, in fact, true. Reality often surprises us. Doug and his wife had a disconnect between their assumptions and reality, a disconnect that was costly.

Design thinking can be particularly useful for couples. The process can identify hypotheses that each partner has around living options and create a method to test them. Perhaps one partner would like to move to an age-restricted community and the other would like to stay put. Identify the reasons for moving and not moving. Tease out the underlying hypotheses for each person's point of view. The couple may be at a stalemate, or there could be a test to uncover a false hypothesis. Suppose the partner interested in staying put assumes that age-restricted communities are insular. This hypothesis could be tested by talking to more people, doing online research, and visiting an age-restricted community. It would be more valuable to participate in an event in the community or rent a unit for a period of time to try it out.

As you evaluate options, carefully think through and prioritize implicit assumptions for each place. Determine your confidence about each hypothesis, and list ideas to test whether your hypothesis is correct. Enlist support from friends and family as desired. This exercise may help with your thinking even without testing your assumptions. It may help you understand the risk and the factors that really matter to you.

Investment in making sure you are making the right move is almost always well spent, particularly when the decision is difficult to reverse.

MANAGING THE MOVE, HANDLING THE TRANSITION, AND EMBRACING THE NEW ENVIRONMENT

Making the decision to move and identifying where to move are huge accomplishments. In some respects, though, the adventure has just begun. The execution of a move and the transition, particularly for older adults who have not moved in some time, can be a major ordeal.

If you are selling a house, follow industry best practices to optimize speed and value. One thing to consider, particularly if you have an older house with dated decor, is to stage your house with contemporary furniture to help buyers better envision the space. If you have a house that could be renovated or expanded, you can meet with architects and builders to get a sense of what possible changes within certain budgets. You can then share this information with potential buyers to help them envision how the space could be changed with incremental investment. Be sure to choose a real estate broker who has relationships in the buyer community for your type of home and is tech-savvy. Make sure your agent is aware of your preferences regarding timing, pricing, and assurance of a transaction. Holding up your transition because of a miscommunication with your agent is an avoidable mistake.

Right-sizing your possessions will be part of the process, as discussed in chapter 14. Understand your current needs, and determine which items should be part of your next chapter. Odds are that it is less than you think. Focus on items that give you joy. Use this time as an opportunity to digitize keepsakes to preserve memories.

Moving is emotional. The process will affect each of us differently and at different times. Our response to these emotions can be aggravated by the stress of moving. Some of the emotions may be positive, such as a recollection of fond memories in our home. Invariably, moving evokes a feeling of sadness and loss, and recognition of a chapter of life closed. These feelings can be especially strong if you are leaving a long-term home and if you feel pushed to a new setting. Recognize that your emotions may be different than your partner's.

Emotions can be amplified if you are going through the process alone. A friend's mom sold her house after living in it for more than 40 years, the last 10 alone after her husband passed away from cancer. She had purchased and outfitted a condo apartment, and until the sale closed, she spent every night in her house, even though the only furniture remaining was in her bedroom and kitchen. She wanted to savor every last moment.

Seek help in downsizing and moving. Make an event out of it. Invite friends to help in the process, and break it down into digestible chunks. Don't be afraid to lean on family during this time. If family members are out of town, encourage them to visit to help. It is easy to underestimate all the pressures of a move, particularly if you are alone or haven't moved in some time. Conserve energy, including emotional energy, wherever possible, as the energy needed on the other side is often much more than you would expect.

Timing a move from one home to another can be tricky. Sometimes, there is a sizeable gap between leaving one permanent residence and moving into another. It's important to create a buffer. Particularly when a move involves a major change in geography, logistics are complicated and uncontrollable to some degree. Odds are unlikely that everything works out as hoped. A home purchase may fall through. There may be a hiccup with the availability of your apartment. Your possessions might get delayed in transition. The possibilities are endless. Advanced planning is more important for hard-to-sell homes.

Particularly in situations that involve many moving parts, it can be wise to set up temporary residence. It could be a short-term rental, hotel, or staying with a friend or family. Having a plan on the front end can ease the stress of the overall situation.

Whether the impetus for change was a pull toward an attractive environment or a push out of a home that was no longer appropriate, embrace the new living situation. The eventual outcome of moving your new environment will be highly influenced by your attitude toward it, starting from the beginning.

One of the exciting elements of a move is that you start with a clean slate. Your habits and routines have been disrupted. A fresh start presents an opportunity to create new habits and routines and align them with important priorities. Environmental triggers can make habits—both good and bad—easy to create. You can design your new environment to nudge you toward healthier habits; it could be as simple as removing the TV from your bedroom to cut down on screen time to creating a dedicated spot for exercise.

Consider how a move can enhance well-being. Seek opportunities for more purpose, like volunteering in the community. Take advantage of opportunities for greater physical activity. Perhaps you have access to a gym or walking paths. Use the transition as an opportunity to get into a habit of daily activity.

Social connection can be elusive in the beginning. For those who value community, which they may have had in their old place, the early days of a transition can be rough. It's hard to make best friends immediately. It takes time, repeated encounters, and shared interests. It's important to be patient.

In general, err on the side of saying "yes" and trying things out when you enter a new environment. By putting yourself out there, you will learn what and who you like. You can think of it as applying design thinking principles. Create experiments and see which ones work. You may be pleasantly surprised and feel energized about the new environment.

The transition can be particularly challenging when moving into senior living environments. This is because the senior living model is predicated on people living amongst each other. Personal space is often minimal, and there is an expectation to be involved in programming offered at the community. For new residents transitioning from a private residence, an adjustment can take time.

The transition to a retirement community was initially difficult for my friend Dick. He lost his wife, and as his health deteriorated, he wanted to be in a living environment that provided support when he needed it. Moving into his retirement community was awkward.

There weren't many men, and most were married. Finding friends was not easy at first. He kept to himself but started to meet people through meals. Before too long, he joined activities, including the weekly men's poker game. He started to make friends and became busy, sometimes too busy to field calls from his family. It ended up being a great fit, despite it not feeling that way initially.

The bottom line is that transitions are almost always challenging. Set realistic expectations. Be cognizant that emotions may run high for a few months or longer. Be patient and be yourself.

SPECIAL CONSIDERATIONS FOR CLOSE FRIENDS AND FAMILY, INCLUDING ADULT CHILDREN

The best situation is when a loved one recognizes the need for change and chooses a new place. Friends and family may only be needed to double-check the wisdom of the decision and assist with the move and transition. Unfortunately, few cases follow this description.

More often than not, a change is triggered by a health event, such as a fall or a stroke. When this happens, friends and family may need to take a leading or co-leading role in finding a new living environment for their loved one. This task can be urgent and important and may require dropping other responsibilities to address it promptly and properly.

A loved one's life is rarely in complete order. A house may not be prepped for a sale. Belongings may be too numerous and disorganized. Financial information may be in disarray. End-of-life preferences, health care directives, power of attorney, and so on may be incomplete. More than anything, a loved one may not be emotionally prepared for a change. There may be a lot for friends and family to understand and triage.

The transition to a new place can be fraught for older adults who did not advocate for a change. Emotions run high. The move from a primary residence of decades may trigger one cascade of emotions that are entirely separate from those triggered when moving to a new location not of one's choosing. Emotional damage can be caused in the decision making and the transition. Friends and family must proceed carefully, and still the process may end with regrets.

A friend, Anthony, managed a change in location for his mother, one that he would do differently today if offered the chance. Anthony is South African, and he lives with his wife and family in the San Francisco Bay Area. Anthony's mom was living in South Africa and struggling with her health. It was clear that her living environment could not support her, and Anthony felt it would be better if she lived near him and his family for support. The challenge was that her social network was in South Africa. The collective decision was to have his mother move from South Africa to a senior living community in the San Francisco Bay Area.

The move was difficult given the distance and cultural differences. What made things more challenging was the transition. She missed her friends and support network in South Africa, and Anthony, while loving and accessible, had a full plate of responsibilities between his work and family. For his mom, there was a gap between the desired frequency of seeing her son and his family and the practical realities of the situation. The situation was made worse by the cultural differences in her new environment. She wasn't of a mindset to make friends and consequently didn't. Anthony wonders whether it would have been better for his mom to stay in South Africa and move into a retirement community with her friends.

In cases of dementia care for a loved one, the responsibilities for adult children are substantial. Adult children drive the decision making. Dementia care communities can be expensive, as can around-the-clock care at a single-family house. Finding the right solution is critical, but the set of feasible options is often small.

Adult children must understand that a move to a senior living community may not be the last move. Depending on changes in health and financial resources, additional moves may be necessary. It could be a move to a skilled nursing facility or a move in with family. Each move presents risks, challenges, and adjustments.

CHECKLIST FOR NEXT STEPS

If you plan is to move from your current home, below is a checklist of factors to consider:

☐ Develop a process and timeline for determining the right next place. If you have a partner or spouse, engage in developing a plan together. Outline elements that matter to each person, and create an initial list of possible candidates. Be sure to thoughtfully consider preferences and fears as well as the underlying hypotheses driving these perspectives.

☐ Consider regional, metropolitan, and neighborhood factors in addition to built environments. It is better to start broad and narrow to a set of options than to limit your universe to a small set of options within your current existing geographic area. Particularly if you plan to be a part of the workforce for an extended time, appreciate the importance of being a part of a dynamic local economy.

☐ Gain an appreciation for the constraints impacting your decision, such as those related to finances, health, and extended family. Don't waste time considering options that are not grounded in reality.

☐ Give yourself time, measured in months or years ideally, to think through options in greater detail, and apply design thinking principles to test whether a potential option is what you really want.

☐ Determine a path forward and solicit input from friends, family, and professionals when desired. It is helpful to get insights from those who love you to validate the sanity of your decision making. It is also valuable to get feedback from investment advisors, as well as attorneys and health care professionals, particularly if you are looking into a move into senior living.

☐ Manage the move with realistic expectations. Right-size possessions, keeping those that provide utility and joy. Seek help from friends and family to support you during the process.

☐ Set realistic expectations about the nature of the transition. Changes of any type, particularly as we get older, can be challenging. Expect things not to go as planned, and create a buffer in case of an unexpected event. In some cases, you may need to arrange temporary housing until the new home is available and the transition is complete.

☐ Embrace the new environment, and be patient. Look for ways to experience your new environment as fully as possible, such as meeting new neighbors and engaging in what the lifestyle offers. Take advantage of the new environment to create new habits that align with your life goals and overall well-being. Also recognize that it will take some time, measured at least in months, before you feel settled. Note that you may feel physically settled before feeling emotionally settled.

Use this checklist for managing a move or transition on behalf of a loved one:

☐ Work with your loved one to understand what their preferred place looks like. Help them brainstorm potential options and test-drive options if time allows. It is important to make a decision that generates positive emotions about the possibilities of the new environment, even if there is a sadness about leaving home. Hire professionals, such as a certified senior advisor (CSA), to help identify the best options and navigate the process.

☐ Make sure the new place meets the requirements for your loved one. This includes financial, health, and family considerations. Gain insights from other friends and family as well as professionals, such as investment advisors, attorneys, health care professionals, and CSAs. Your loved one should own the decision and see positives of the move to the greatest possible extent. In the case of moves into senior living, research shows that a lack of agency in the decision to move results in older adults being less engaged in social activities.[2]

☐ Lead the moving and downsizing process. Be emotionally sensitive to the needs of your loved one. Utilize digital tools, particularly when communicating and coordinating with multiple groups.

☐ Manage the transition or hire professionals so that it is as smooth as possible for your loved one. Recognize that hiccups will occur during the transition process, and be available for your loved one, providing ad hoc support where needed. Help make sure the new environment is set up for success, including, but not limited to, the layout of furniture and implementation of technology.

☐ Work with and stay in regular communication with your loved one. Encourage them to embrace their new environment and focus on its positives. The ability of a loved one to see their new place as their new home is a key benefit for all involved. Particularly if the environment is care centric, like assisted living or dementia care, introduce yourself to the leadership of the care team to establish yourself as an advocate for your loved one.

CONCLUSION

A decision to move is significant at any age. For older adults, inertia can be a particularly powerful force. A move is often triggered by the prospect of a better life (i.e., being "pulled" into a new environment) or the realization that the current environment is no longer appropriate (i.e., being "pushed" out of an existing home).

The decision to move is not enough; success depends on selecting the right place, successfully managing the transition, and embracing the new environment. Don't expect every step to go perfectly. Patience and flexibility are key character traits during this process.

The adage that the only constant is change is something to keep in mind. Making a big move, even if it means moving into a retirement community, may not be the final change of place. Things can occur that make the current environment no longer the best place, again triggering the whole process of finding the right place, moving, transitioning, and embracing the new environment. The hope is that this process doesn't happen often, but not being open to change when change is needed can be the worst scenario of all.

CHOOSING THE RIGHT PLACE
AT THE RIGHT TIME

For me, spending time in nature is the best reminder of the power of place. I have backpacked with a handful of close friends each year for the past decade or so, most times in the backcountry of Yosemite National Park. What started as an unconventional bachelor party has become an annual ritual. We've fished in mountain lakes, swum in pools of water leading to waterfalls, and soaked in glorious vistas. It hasn't all been smooth, however. We've been caught off guard by hailstorms, nearly catching hypothermia; crossed snowmelt rivers that reached our midsections, holding backpacks above our heads; and been served up as an all-you-can eat buffet for tenacious mosquitos.

Our lives have mirrored the peaks and valleys of the terrain we've covered. We've celebrated marriages, births of children, and career accomplishments. At times it has even felt like we've solved the world's problems, no doubt aided by a campfire and scotch. Yet we also have endured hardships, like a spouse succumbing to cancer in her 30s, deterioration of health and eventual loss of parents, and the challenges of having and raising children.

Our annual pilgrimage to the mountains serves to amplify the highs and cushion the lows. Our friendships play a role, but so does the backdrop of Mother Nature's beauty. There's something about being in the outdoors that offers peaceful clarity on what matters most. It provides a perspective and grounding that puts our joys and trials into a broader context. It's also a reminder of how the right place can ease our anxieties and help us thrive.

THE COMPLEXITY OF SOLVING FOR PLACE

Longevity is a gift of our modern times. It's one that not all of us get to unwrap. The opportunity to be healthy and financially secure into our 70s and beyond is a combination of good fortune and wise choices.

Place is among the choices that matter. Implicit is that place is *our* choice. There may be options that others deem safe or appropriate, but assuming we are not endangering others and have economic means, we have the freedom to choose what's best for us.

This freedom comes with responsibility. It requires self-knowledge. You need to be aware of which environments you thrive in, and which ones crush your spirit. Only you know when place is right.

This doesn't mean that analytics and planning don't have a place. They most certainly do. While people change, so do places. It's complex solving for two dynamic variables.

Some changes to place are predictable. Economic trends favor some places over others. Climate change puts some locations at risk. Debt and demographics have an effect on growth. Other changes are unpredictable. Some of us may have intellectually understood the risk of a pandemic, but few were prepared for the way COVID-19 upended life. Natural disasters strike. Political upheaval and revolutions happen. Economic crashes occur.

Recognizing that places change is important for planning. It means that we should be careful making unconditional commitments to a place. How we think of place ought to have some ability to change as circumstances change. This can happen in the macro (our area isn't the place it used to be) and it can happen in the micro (our house is falling apart).

We also struggle with the other part of the formula: us. We can inadvertently convince ourselves that we are immortal and have control of our fate. Yet tomorrow may not come. If it does, it may be different than we anticipate. We are surprised at times when we shouldn't be. We know with 100% certainty that a time will come when we won't be here.

Beyond matters of mortality, there is the likelihood that our life span will not match our health span and wealth span. Try as we may, it's difficult to have these three elements line up exactly. Our health needs and financial constraints may affect our options for place. If we ignore changes in life's circumstances, it won't insulate us from the risks. Lack of planning and unawareness of reality heighten the odds of being in the wrong place. Living in the wrong place negatively affects well-being.

When health changes, there can be a tendency for care needs to dictate place. While this can come from a place of love and concern on behalf of others to keep us safe, safety may not be the driving force behind your motivation. It's important to know what matters most to you so that when faced with trade-offs, you know what path to follow. It may be a less safe place, but one that you love. This is part of Bob's motivation for staying put in his single-family home.

Solving for place is complex and dynamic. There is no one right answer, but some answers are better than others. Doing the work to determine the right place matters, because place has such a profound impact on our well-being.

ANOTHER APPROACH: COMMITMENT TO PLACE

In some cases, a choice of place can transform into a steadfast commitment to place. In essence, we merge with our place, and uprooting ourselves becomes incredibly painful, if not impossible. Author, poet, and environmentalist Wendell Berry sums it up when he says:

> And so I came to belong to this place. Being here satisfies me.
> I had laid my claim on the place and had made it answerable

to my life. Of course you can't do that and get away free. You can't choose it seems without being chosen. For the place in return had laid its claim on me and had made my life answerable to it.[1]

I admire people who have committed to a place, particularly where they have invested in their communities for the better. These people tend to benefit from deep relationships and a strong support network. While the passage of time is helpful, these people need not have spent their entire life in one location. This commitment to place can happen later in life, but it does require intentionality.

Fred and Carol Smith made a commitment to place in their mid-30s. While passing through East Texas, Fred had a premonition the region would be their future home. His vision was accurate. After stops in the West and Northeast, the Smiths relocated to Tyler, Texas, a city about 100 miles southeast of Dallas. When they moved in the 1980s, the population was approximately 75,000 people. Today, it exceeds 100,000.

The Smiths moved for a job opportunity for Fred, but they sensed something more significant was afoot. Tyler represented a community large enough to attract interesting people and support growing organizations, but small enough to get to know others personally and be able to make a tangible impact. Fred later left the job that brought them to Tyler and switched to a role focused on community building. For more than three decades, Fred and Carol, separately and together, have invested in relationships and causes to help make Tyler a better place. Their efforts have had an impact on public schools, not-for-profits, women's circles, business networks, churches, and more. For the place of Tyler, the Smiths are examples of what David Brooks calls weavers.

Now in their 70s, Fred and Carol have no intention of leaving Tyler. They can't. Their ties are too strong. Their story is too interwoven with that of their community. Place has laid claim on them. Their opportunity is to continue to live in community as they age.

DEVELOPING THE DISCIPLINE OF CHOOSING
THE RIGHT PLACE AT THE RIGHT TIME

Regular calibration is necessary to make sure you are in the right place at the right time. Herein lies the problem with aging in place. It often does not adequately account for the realities of change around us. Some people who age in place pretend that change does not occur, and as though determination alone will allow them to power through regardless of circumstance. Rarely is this the proper course.

We evaluate place during times of transition. A job change may trigger a potential move. The end of a marriage or loss of a spouse may also mean a change of place. A change in one's health may require the same. When these life transitions occur, questions like, "Am I in the right place?" percolate naturally.

The trick is to be aware of when calibration is necessary during the normal course of life. Observation and attunement are key. Notice how place is changing around you. Maybe there is turnover in your neighborhood and increased traffic. These can be positive signs for growth in your area, but they may negatively affect your life. Maybe you sense a change in what you value in life. The large garden that once brought joy becomes a chore. The idea of a smaller garden with less to maintain gains appeal.

The lives of friends and peers can be instructive. A friend downsizes and loves her decision. Another friend remodels her home to make it conducive to aging, and the approach seems to be working. A separate friend is caught off guard with a health event and struggles to find the best new place. Lessons from others can influence your strategy in what to do and what not to do.

Consider modifying rituals to prompt the question of place. If you practice New Year's resolutions, consider adding a standing question about the role of place. If you get together as an extended family each year, use the gathering to talk about place for each person. Adult children can use this as an opportunity to raise questions or concerns with a loved one as part of a normal course of life, rather than in response to a crisis.

If the process of assessing one's situation reveals opportunities for improvement, a change in place may not be necessary. A tweak can make a difference. Find friends to walk with regularly. Volunteer for a cause that matters to you. Add grab bars to the bathroom. Don't let the fear of change dissuade you from taking regular stock as to whether you are in the right spot.

CLOSING THOUGHT: A CALL TO ACTION FOR OUR SOCIETY

The opportunity for place to enrich our lives is omnipresent. We need to be aware of its impact, assess the appropriateness of our current environment, and have the courage to take action when needed. The formula is simple.

Each of us can do more to help those around us. We can help family, friends, and acquaintances think more about the role of place in their lives. We can ask them how they think about place, and remind them about its direct and indirect impacts on our lives. It can be positioned less as fear, and more as an opportunity for a better life. It's even better if we offer a helping hand in the process.

The opportunity to help extends beyond our social networks. There is an advocacy role to help make our communities age-friendly. More people of all ages need to speak out about the needs of older adults and encourage policy changes. The crushing impact of COVID-19 on older adults is a reminder that we can and should do better as a society to help people thrive across the course of life.

Ageism—the stereotyping and discrimination against individuals or groups on the basis of their age—does not help.[2] Ageism makes older people think less of themselves and young people overlook the benefits of being older. It is a form of discrimination against ourselves. Anti-ageism activist Ashton Applewhite points out that with ageism, "we are discriminating against our future selves."[3]

Place can perpetuate ageism. We lose richness in our communities when people of all ages are not present. We deny young people the opportunity to see what old age is like—recall that the happiest people are the oldest—and older people miss out on the vitality of youth. Without intergenerational relationships, young people are more easily seduced by the false promises of youth, and older people lose the opportunity for greater purpose in mentoring younger people.

A societal goal should be to make it easier for people to live in their preferred place at each point in life. At the same time, we should also make it easier for people of all ages to live proximate to each other. The opportunity is not just to make our own lives better through wise choices for place; we can also create more attractive options for place for people of all ages. Collectively, we can make this vision possible.

We have an opportunity to broaden how we think about place. Our annual backpacking trip in 2020 was canceled because of the coronavirus. So we improvised. We created a virtual community, using video and text to communicate regularly, provide updates on our lives, and crack jokes. We looked at pictures of past trips, exchanged outdoor websites, and shared passages from books that capture the feeling of the outdoors. In a sense, we were able to transport ourselves to our desired place. We just needed to be creative.

Creativity is what we all need to tap into the power of place. The right home for one stage may be wrong for another. Some solutions will be obvious, others less so. We mustn't forget the importance of place at any age. Place influences well-being in direct and indirect ways, and it deserves special attention. If, as a society, we make better decisions about place and create more attractive options, many more of us will successfully embrace the fullness of living in the Age of Longevity.

PERSONAL DASHBOARDS

Your Personal Dashboard

Purpose	0	FULL
Social Connection	0	FULL
Physical Well-Being	0	FULL
Financial Well-Being	0	FULL
Place	0	FULL

Your Partner's Personal Dashboard

Purpose	0	FULL
Social Connection	0	FULL
Physical Well-Being	0	FULL
Financial Well-Being	0	FULL
Place	0	FULL

RESOURCES

AARP Livability Index (https://livabilityindex.aarp.org/). An index curated by the AARP Public Policy Institute that helps individuals and policymakers determine the livability of a community down to the neighborhood. Can be a useful tool to get a sense of the livability of your current home or prospective places of interest.

AARP Livable Communities (https://www.aarp.org/livable-communities/network-age-friendly-communities/). Provides a list of cities, towns, and counties as well as states and territories that are part of the AARP Network of Age-Friendly States and Communities.

Congress for the New Urbanism (cnu.org). An organization committed to helping create more great walkable urban places. Provides resources, including a list of projects underway or completed, that embrace their principles.

Long-Term Services and Supports State Scorecard (https://www.longtermscorecard.org/). Pulls together publicly available information to compare states in their ability to help older adults through long-term care and supports.

Mercatus Center at George Mason University (https://www.mercatus.org/publications/urban-economics/state-fiscal-rankings). Publishes a comparison and ranking of states by overall fiscal health.

Milken Institute Center for the Future of Aging (https://milkeninstitute .org/centers/center-for-the-future-of-aging). Offers reports, data, and insights on specific geographies that are well positioned to support successful aging.

Smart Growth America (www.smartgrowthamerica.org). Publishes reports and data on regions, states, and metropolitan areas that are pursuing smart growth strategies, including complete street policies and the development of walkable urban or suburban areas.

Tax Foundation (www.taxfoundation.org). The leading independent tax policy nonprofit. Publishes data that compares tax polices across states.

SINGLE-FAMILY HOMES

Community Aging in Place–Advancing Better Living for Elders (https:// nursing.jhu.edu/faculty_research/research/projects/capable/index .html). Helps low-income seniors to safely age in place in their communities. CAPABLE currently operates in 17 states but is expected to expand.

National Association of Home Builders (https://www.nahb.org/). Provides resources to learn more about the home building industry, including trends. You can find Certified Aging in Place Specialists (CAPS) by searching the NAHB directory.

APARTMENTS

Apartments.com (www.apartments.com). A consumer site to help identify apartment properties in a given area. Can filter by age to narrow search to age-restricted apartment buildings.

National Multifamily Housing Council (www.nmhc.org). Provides resources to learn more about apartments, including information about leading owners and operators.

SENIOR LIVING AND SENIOR SERVICES

American Seniors Housing Association (https://www.seniorshousing .org/). Provides resources to better understand the senior living field, including its consumer resource Where You Live Matters (whereyoulivematters.org).

Centers for Medicaid and Medicare Services (medicare.gov/care -compare). Service that utilizes public information to compare the quality of a number of health care service providers, ranging from skilled nursing homes to home health services to rehabilitation facilities and more. Uses a five-star system to evaluate skilled nursing homes.

Society of Certified Senior Advisors (csa.us). Provides helpful information for older adults and their families, including a directory of certified senior advisors (CSAs) across the country.

EMERGING MODELS

Cohousing Association of America (https://www.cohousing.org/). Provides basic information on cohousing and how to get involved. Includes information about age-restricted cohousing locations.

Senior Cooperative Foundation (seniorcoops.org). A nonprofit that provides information on co-ops, including a list of communities across the country.

HOME MODIFICATION

AARP Home Fit Guide (https://www.aarp.org/livable-communities /housing/info-2020/homefit-guide.html). Guide to help individuals and their families make their current or future residence a lifelong home.

Universal Design Living Laboratory (www.udll.com). Provides a tool kit and resources to get the latest information on universal design standards and implementation approaches.

NOTES

INTRODUCTION. WHY PLACE MATTERS IN THE AGE OF LONGEVITY

1. Renee Stepler, "World's Centenarian Population Projected to Grow Eightfold by 2050," Pew Research Center, April 21, 2016, https://www.pewresearch.org /fact-tank/2016/04/21/worlds-centenarian-population-projected-to-grow -eightfold-by-2050/.

2. Lynda Gratton and Andrew Scott, *The 100-Year Life: Living and Working in an Age of Longevity* (Bloomsbury Information, 2016).

3. "The U-Bend of Life," *Economist*, December 16, 2010.

4. Genetics Society of Aging, "Family Tree of 400 Million People Shows Genetics Has Limited Influence on Longevity," Medical Press, November 6, 2018, https://med icalxpress.com/news/2018-11-family-tree-million-people-genetics.html.

5. Laura L. Carstensen, PhD, *A Long Bright Future: An Action Plan for a Lifetime of Happiness, Health, and Financial Security* (Harmony, 2009), chap. 2.

6. "The 'Loneliness Epidemic,'" Health Resources and Services Administration, January 17, 2019, https://www.hrsa.gov/enews/past-issues/2019/january -17/loneliness-epidemic.

7. "New Cigna Study Reveals Loneliness at Epidemic Levels in America," Cigna, May 1, 2018, https://www.cigna.com/about-us/newsroom/news-and-views/press -releases/2018/new-cigna-study-reveals-loneliness-at-epidemic-levels-in-america.

8. John Templeton Foundation, *The Psychology of Purpose* (John Templeton Foundation, 2018), https://www.templeton.org/wp-content/uploads/2020/02 /Psychology-of-Purpose.pdf.

9. Dan Buettner, *The Blue Zones: Lessons for Living Longer from the People Who've Lived the Longest* (National Geographic, 2010).

10. Carole Despres and Sébastien Lord, "Growing Older in Postwar Suburbs: The Meanings and Experiences of Home," in *Home and Identity in Later Life: International Perspectives*, ed. Graham D. Rowles and Habib Chaudhury (Springer, 2005), 317–40.

11. Raj Chetty, Michael Stepner, Sarah Abraham, Shelby Lin, Benjamin Scuderi, Nicholas Turner, Augustin Bergeron, and David Cutler, "The Association between Income and Life Expectancy in the United States, 2001–2014," *JAMA* 315, no. 16 (2016): 1750–66, doi:10.1001/jama.2016.4226.

12. "Calculating Migration Expectancy Using ACS Data," US Census Bureau, last revised July 18, 2020, https://www.census.gov/topics/population/migration /guidance/calculating-migration-expectancy.html.

13. Sara Zeff Geber, *Essential Retirement Planning for Solo Agers: A Retirement and Aging Roadmap for Single and Childless Adults* (Mango, 2018).

CHAPTER 1. PLACE AS A KEY COMPONENT OF SUCCESSFUL AGING

1. Tom Rath and Jim Harter, *Wellbeing: The Five Essential Elements* (Gallup Press, 2010). Note that I replace the author's phrase *career wellbeing* with *purpose*, which is a more broadly defining term and one that may better reflect people who are past their primary career stage.

2. Gallup defines community well-being as liking where you live, feeling safe, and having pride in your community.

3. Carol S. Dweck, *Mindset: The New Psychology of Success* (Random House, 2006).

4. "Charlotte Siegel: Winner of the CSCSW Award for Contributions to the Field of Social Work," California Society for Clinical Social Work, February 13, 2017, https://www.clinicalsocialworksociety.org/announcements/4607520.

5. John Templeton Foundation, *The Psychology of Purpose* (John Templeton Foundation, 2018), chap. 3, https://www.templeton.org/wp-content/uploads /2020/02/Psychology-of-Purpose.pdf.

6. John Templeton Foundation, *Psychology of Purpose*.

7. John Templeton Foundation, *Psychology of Purpose*.

8. John Templeton Foundation, *Psychology of Purpose*.

9. John Templeton Foundation, *Psychology of Purpose*.

10. Marc Freedman, *Encore: Finding Work That Matters in the Second Half of Life* (PublicAffairs, 2007).

11. Vivek Murthy, "Work and the Loneliness Epidemic," *Harvard Business Review*, September 26, 2017, https://hbr.org/2017/09/work-and-the-loneliness-epidemic.

12. Julianne Holt-Lunstad, Timothy B. Smith, Mark Baker, Tyler Harris, and David Stephenson, "Loneliness and Social Isolation as Risk Factors for Mortality: A Meta-Analytic Review," *Perspectives on Psychological Science* 10, no. 2 (2015): 227–37, doi:10.1177/1745691614568352.

13. Tim Adams, "John Cacioppo: 'Loneliness Is Like an Iceberg—It Goes Deeper Than We Can See,'" *The Guardian*, February 28, 2016, https://www.theguardian.com /science/2016/feb/28/loneliness-is-like-an-iceberg-john-cacioppo-social-neuro science-interview.

14. "Social Isolation, Loneliness in Older People Pose Health Risks," National Institute on Aging, April 23, 2019, https://www.nia.nih.gov/news/social-isolation -loneliness-older-people-pose-health-risks#:~:text=Social%20isolation%20is%20 the%20objective,alone%20yet%20not%20feel%20lonely.

15. "Social Isolation, Loneliness in Older People Pose Health Risks."

16. Susan Pinker, *The Village Effect: How Face-to-Face Contact Can Make Us Healthier and Happier* (Spiegel & Grau, 2015).

17. Holly B. Shakya and Nicholas A. Christakis, "A New, More Rigorous Study Confirms: The More You Use Facebook, the Worse You Feel," *Harvard Business Review*, April 10, 2017, https://hbr.org/2017/04/a-new-more-rigorous-study -confirms-the-more-you-use-facebook-the-worse-you-feel.

18. For more information, visit the Sufferfest website: www.sufferfest.net.

19. Gretchen Reynolds, "Exercise Makes the Aging Heart More Youthful," *New York Times*, July 25, 2018, https://www.nytimes.com/2018/07/25/well/exercise -makes-the-aging-heart-more-youthful.html.

20. Gretchen Reynolds, "Even a 10-Minute Walk May Be Good for the Brain," *New York Times*, October 24, 2018, https://www.nytimes.com/2018/10/24/well /move/exercise-brain-memory-fitness-cognitive.html.

21. Gretchen Reynolds, "The Right Kind of Exercise May Boost Memory and Lower Dementia Risk," *New York Times*, November 6, 2019, https://www.nytimes .com/2019/11/06/well/move/exercise-dementia-memory-alzheimers-brain -seniors-middle-age.html.

22. Nicholas Bakalar, "The Healthier Your Heart, The Healthier Your Brain May Be," *New York Times*, August 21, 2018, https://www.nytimes.com/2018/08/21/well /mind/the-healthier-your-heart-the-healthier-your-brain-may-be.html.

23. Gretchen Reynolds, "How Weight Training Changes the Brain," *New York Times*, July 24, 2019, https://www.nytimes.com/2019/07/24/well/move/how -weight-training-changes-the-brain.html.

24. Gretchen Reynolds, "The Best Sport for a Longer Life? Try Tennis," *New York Times*, September 5, 2018, https://www.nytimes.com/2018/09/05/well/move/the -best-sport-for-a-longer-life-try-tennis.html.

25. GDB 2017 Diet Collaborators, "Health Effects of Dietary Risks in 195 Countries, 1990–2017: A Systematic Analysis for the Global Burden of Disease Study 2017," *The Lancet* 393, no. 10184 (2019): P1958-1972, doi:https://doi.org/10.1016/S0140-6736(19)30041-8.

26. Jane E. Brody, "Tackling Inflammation to Fight Age-Related Ailments," *New York Times*, December 23, 2019, https://www.nytimes.com/2019/12/23/well/live/inflammation-aging-age-heart-disease-cancer-alzheimers-dementia-diabetes-depression-health.html.

27. Anne Tergesen, "What Science Tells Us about Preventing Dementia," *Wall Street Journal*, November 17, 2019, https://www.wsj.com/articles/what-science-tells-us-about-preventing-dementia-11574004600.

28. Matthew Walker, *Why We Sleep: Unlocking the Power of Sleep and Dreams* (Scribner, 2017).

29. Heather Murphy, "Rich People Don't Just Live Longer. They Also Get More Healthy Years," *New York Times*, January 16, 2020, https://www.nytimes.com/2020/01/16/science/rich-people-longer-life-study.html.

30. "Analysis of the 2020 Social Security Trustees' Report," Committee for a Responsible Budget, April 22, 2020, http://www.crfb.org/papers/analysis-2020-social-security-trustees-report.

31. "Finances in Retirement: New Challenges, New Solutions: A Capstone Study Culminating a Series of Studies Investigating Retirement," Age Wave, accessed December 1, 2020, https://agewave.com/what-we-do/landmark-research-and-consulting/research-studies/finances-in-retirement-new-challenges-new-solutions/.

32. Tim Herrera, "Why It's So Hard to Put 'Future You' Ahead of 'Present You,'" *New York Times*, September 10, 2018, https://www.nytimes.com/2018/09/10/smarter-living/why-its-so-hard-to-put-future-you-ahead-of-present-you.html.

33. Senator Mike Lee, *A Future Without Kin?* (Washington, DC: US Congress Joint Economic Committee, 2018), https://www.jec.senate.gov/public/index.cfm/republicans/2018/1/a-future-without-kin.

34. "Finances in Retirement."

35. "Finances in Retirement."

36. "Finances in Retirement."

37. Caroline Servat, Nora Super, and Paul Irving, *Age-Forward Cities for 2030* (Milken Institute Center for the Future of Aging, 2019).

38. Joe Kita, "Workplace Age Discrimination Still Flourishes in America," AARP, December 30, 2019, https://www.aarp.org/work/working-at-50-plus/info-2019/age-discrimination-in-america.html.

39. "How Much Care Will You Need?," Administration on Aging, US Department of Health and Human Services, last modified October 15, 2020, https://longterm care.acl.gov/the-basics/how-much-care-will-you-need.html.

40. "Finances in Retirement."

41. Daniel Cox and Ryan Streeter, "Having a Library or Café Down the Block Could Change Your Life," *The Atlantic*, May 20, 2019, https://www.theatlantic.com /ideas/archive/2019/05/america-needs-more-community-spaces/589729/.

42. Ramon Oldenburg and Dennis Brissett, "The Third Place," *Qualitative Sociology* 5 (1982): 265–84, https://doi.org/10.1007/BF00986754.

43. Jessica Finlay, Michael Esposito, Sandra Tang, Iris Gomez-Lopez, Dominique Sylvers, Suzanne Judd, and Philippa Clarke, "Fast-Food for Thought: Retail Food Environments as Resources for Cognitive Health and Wellbeing among Aging Americans?," *Health and Place* 64 (2020): 102379.

44. Generations United and the Eisner Foundation, *All In Together: Creating Places Where Young and Old Thrive* (Generations United and the Eisner Foundation, 2018), https://www.gu.org/app/uploads/2018/06/SignatureReport-Eisner-All-In -Together.pdf.

45. Brett Arends, "Living near Major Roads Linked to Risk of Dementia, Parkinson's, MS," *New York Post*, January 28, 2020, https://nypost.com/2020/01/28 /living-near-major-roads-linked-to-risk-of-dementia-parkinsons-ms/.

46. Centers for Disease Control and Prevention, *2014 State Indicator Report on Physical Activity* (US Department of Health and Human Services, 2014), https:// www.cdc.gov/physicalactivity/downloads/pa_state_indicator_report_2014.pdf.

47. Dan Buettner, *The Blue Zones: Lessons for Living Longer from the People Who've Lived the Longest* (National Geographic, 1994).

48. Bipartisan Policy Center, *Healthy Aging Begins at Home* (Bipartisan Policy Center, 2016), https://bipartisanpolicy.org/report/recommendations-for-healthy-aging/.

49. Bipartisan Policy Center, *Healthy Aging Begins at Home*.

CHAPTER 2. EVALUATING WHETHER YOU ARE IN THE RIGHT PLACE

1. Stephanie A. Hooker, Anjoli Punjabi, Kacey Justesen, Lucas Boyle, and Michelle D. Sherman, "Encouraging Health Behavior Change: Eight Evidence-Based Strategies," *Family Practice Management* 25, no. 2 (2018): 31–36.

2. BJ Fogg, *Tiny Habits: The Small Changes That Change Everything* (New York: Houghton Mifflin Harcourt, 2020).

3. Marc Freedman, *How to Live Forever: The Enduring Power of Connecting the Generations* (PublicAffairs, 2018).

CHAPTER 3. **MOVING FROM AGING IN PLACE TO LIVING IN COMMUNITY**

1. AARP, *2018 Home and Community Preferences Survey: A National Survey of Adults Age 18-Plus* (AARP, 2018), https://www.aarp.org/content/dam/aarp /research/surveys_statistics/liv-com/2018/home-community-preferences-survey .doi.10.26419-2Fres.00231.001.pdf.

2. Alexander Hermann, "More Older Adults Are Living in Lower-Density Neighborhoods," Joint Center for Housing Studies of Harvard University, January 7, 2019, https://www.jchs.harvard.edu/blog/more-older-adults-are-living-in-lower-density -neighborhoods/#:~:text=Households%20headed%20by%20older%20adults,a%20 majority%20of%20the%20population.

3. "Aging in community" and "staying at home" are both common alternative terms that also have limitations. The former uses the passive "aging," while the later uses "staying," which also is passive.

4. Bronwyn Tanner, Cheryl Tilse, and Desleigh de Jonge, "Restoring and Sustaining Home: The Impact of Home Modifications on the Meaning of Home for Older People," *Journal of Housing for the Elderly* 22, no. 3 (2008): 195–215, doi:10.1080/02763890802232048.

5. David Chandler, "The Costs of Aging in Place Remodeling," *Consumer Affairs*, last updated August 15, 2019, https://www.consumeraffairs.com/homeowners /aging-in-place-remodel-costs.html.

6. See the Village to Village Network website: https://www.vtvnetwork.org/.

7. "AARP Network of Age-Friendly States and Communities," AARP, last updated November 19, 2020, https://www.aarp.org/livable-communities/network-age -friendly-communities/info-2014/member-list.html.

8. "The Mayor's Pledge," Milken Institute Center for the Future of Aging, accessed December 1, 2020, http://successfulaging.milkeninstitute.org/mayors -pledge/.

9. Bipartisan Policy Center, *Healthy Aging Begins at Home* (Bipartisan Policy Center, 2016), https://bipartisanpolicy.org/report/recommendations-for-healthy -aging/.

10. "In-Home Care Costs Breakdown," Aging.com, accessed December 1, 2020, https://www.aging.com/in-home-care-costs-breakdown/.

11. Joint Center for Housing Studies of Harvard University, *Housing America's Older Adults 2019* (Joint Center for Housing Studies of Harvard University, 2019), https://www.jchs.harvard.edu/sites/default/files/Harvard_JCHS_Housing _Americas_Older_Adults_2019.pdf.

12. Joint Center for Housing Studies of Harvard University, *Housing America's Older Adults*.

13. Geoff Williams, "How Climate Change Could Impact Your Home Value," *US News and World Report*, March 29, 2019, https://realestate.usnews.com/real-estate/articles/how-climate-change-could-impact-your-home-value.

14. G. Oscar Anderson and Colette E. Thayer, *Loneliness and Social Connections: A National Survey of Adults 45 and Older* (Washington, DC: AARP Foundation, 2018), https://www.aarp.org/content/dam/aarp/research/surveys_statistics/life-leisure/2018/loneliness-social-connections-2018.doi.10.26419-2Fres.00246.001.pdf.

15. Charles Vogl, *The Art of Community: Seven Principles for Belonging* (Berrett-Koehler, 2016).

CHAPTER 4. REGIONS, STATES, AND METRO AREAS

1. Centers for Disease Control and Prevention, *2014 State Indicator Report on Physical Activity* (US Department of Health and Human Services, 2014), https://www.cdc.gov/physicalactivity/downloads/pa_state_indicator_report_2014.pdf.

2. Smart Growth America and National Complete Streets Coalition, *Dangerous by Design* (Washington, DC: Smart Growth America, 2020).

3. "State Population Change: 2010 to 2018," US Census Bureau, December 19, 2018, https://www.census.gov/library/visualizations/2018/comm/population-change-2010-2018.html.

4. Jared Walczak, *2020 State Business Tax Climate Index* (Tax Foundation, 2020), https://files.taxfoundation.org/20191021155857/2020-State-Business-Tax-Climate-Index-PDF.pdf.

5. Katherine Loughead, "State Individual Income Tax Rates and Brackets for 2020," Tax Foundation, February 4, 2020, https://taxfoundation.org/state-individual-income-tax-rates-and-brackets-for-2020/.

6. "Ranking the States by Fiscal Condition 2018 Edition," Mercatus Center, George Mason University, October 9, 2018, https://www.mercatus.org/publications/urban-economics/state-fiscal-rankings.

7. Susan Reinhard, Jean Accius, Ari Houser, Kathleen Ujvari, Julia Alexis, and Wendy Fox-Grage, *Picking Up the Pace of Change: A State Scorecard on Long-Term Services and Supports for Older Adults, People with Physical Disabilities, and Family Caregivers* (AARP Public Policy Institute, 2017).

8. Jana Lynott, Rodney Harrell, Shannon Guzman, and Brad Gudzinas, *The Livability Index 2018: Transforming Communities for All Ages* (AARP Public Policy Institute, 2018).

9. Sindhu Kubendran, Liana Soll, and Paul Irving, *Best Cities for Successful Aging 2017* (Milken Institute Center for the Future of Aging, 2017), https://milkeninstitute .org/reports/best-cities-successful-aging-2017.

10. There are about 40 cities with a population of 500,000 and above.

11. There are more than 250 cities with a population of less than 500,000 and above 100,000.

12. "Age-Friendly Health Systems Initiative," John A. Hartford Foundation, accessed January 12, 2021, https://www.johnahartford.org/grants-strategy/current -strategies/age-friendly/age-friendly-health-systems-initiative.

13. Tracy Hadden Loh, Christopher B. Leinberger, and Jordan Chafetz, *Foot Traffic Ahead: Ranking Walkable Urbanism in America's Largest Metros* (Washington, DC: George Washington University School of Business and Smart Growth America, 2019).

14. Smart Growth America and National Complete Streets Coalition, *The Best Complete Streets Policies of 2018* (Washington, DC: Smart Growth America, 2018).

15. Smart Growth America and National Complete Streets Coalition, *Dangerous By Design*.

16. Sally Abrahms, "Is Springfield, Mass. the Best Place in America to Grow Old?," Next Avenue, October 31, 2019, https://www.nextavenue.org/springfield-mass-best -place-to-grow-old/.

17. AARP Foundation, *Loneliness and Social Connections: A National Survey of Adults 45 and Older* (AARP Foundation, 2018).

18. Kim Parker, Juliana Menasce Horowitz, Anna Brown, Richard Fry, D'Vera Cohn, and Ruth Igielnik, "What Unites and Divides Urban, Suburban and Rural Communities," Pew Research Center, May 22, 2018, https://www.pewsocialtrends .org/2018/05/22/what-unites-and-divides-urban-suburban-and-rural-communities/.

19. Loh et al., *Foot Traffic Ahead*.

20. Joint Center for Housing Studies of Harvard University, *Housing America's Older Adults 2019* (Joint Center for Housing Studies of Harvard University, 2019), https://www.jchs.harvard.edu/sites/default/files/Harvard_JCHS_Housing _Americas_Older_Adults_2019.pdf.

CHAPTER 5. NEIGHBORHOOD AND COMMUNITIES

1. Lesli Davis and Kim Parker, "A Half-Century after 'Mister Rogers' Debut, 5 Facts about Neighbors in U.S.," Pew Research Center, August 15, 2019, https://www .pewresearch.org/fact-tank/2019/08/15/facts-about-neighbors-in-u-s/.

2. G. Oscar Anderson and Colette E. Thayer, *Loneliness and Social Connections: A National Survey of Adults 45 and Older* (Washington, DC: AARP Foundation,

2018), https://www.aarp.org/content/dam/aarp/research/surveys_statistics /life-leisure/2018/loneliness-social-connections-2018.doi.10.26419-2Fres.00246 .001.pdf.

3. "These Three Moves Will Help You Stop Feeling Lonely," *Psychology Today*, December 11, 2017, https://www.psychologytoday.com/us/blog/brainstorm/201712 /these-three-moves-will-help-you-stop-feeling-lonely.

4. Anderson and Thayer, *Loneliness and Social Connections*.

5. Sarah Goodyear, "Liking Your Neighbors Could Help Prevent You from Having a Stroke," Bloomberg CityLab, September 19, 2013, https://www.bloomberg .com/news/articles/2013-09-19/liking-your-neighbors-could-help-prevent-you -from-having-a-stroke.

6. Eric Klinenberg, *Heat Wave: A Social Autopsy of Disaster in Chicago* (University of Chicago Press, 2002).

7. Jane Jacobs, *The Death and Life of Great American Cities* (Random House, 1961).

8. Daniel A. Cox and Ryan Streeter, *The Importance of Place: Neighborhood Amenities as a Source of Social Connection and Trust* (American Enterprise Institute, 2019), https://www.aei.org/research-products/report/the-importance-of-place -neighborhood-amenities-as-a-source-of-social-connection-and-trust/.

9. Ji Hie Lee, "Older Adults' Third Places and Perceived Social Connectedness" (PhD diss., Texas A&M University, 2015).

10. Ryan Briggs, "Trading Parking Spots for More Public Space on Philadelphia's Grays Ferry Avenue," Urban Land Institute, April 14, 2016.

11. Jay Walljasper, "How a Florida Beach Town Changed How We Live," *Public Square*, May 14, 2019, https://www.cnu.org/publicsquare/2019/05/14/how-florida -beach-town-changed-how-we-live.

12. "Why a 'Ban' on Single-Family Zoning Could Be a Good Thing," National Association of Home Builders, August 28, 2019, http://nahbnow.com/2019/08 /why-a-ban-on-single-family-zoning-could-be-a-good-thing/.

13. Abigail Murrish, "Porching in Indianapolis," *Comment*, July 3, 2018, https:// www.cardus.ca/comment/article/porching-in-indianapolis/.

14. Maria Neuman, "Why America Is Rediscovering the Social Front Yard," *Wall Street Journal*, June 6, 2020, https://www.wsj.com/articles/why-america-is -rediscovering-the-social-front-yard-11591416037.

15. Scott Calvert, "Creating Bike Lanes Isn't Easy. Just Ask Baltimore. Or Boulder. Or Seattle," *Wall Street Journal*, April 18, 2018, https://www.wsj.com/articles/creating -bike-lanes-isnt-easy-just-ask-baltimore-or-boulder-or-seattle-1524043800.

16. Donald F. Schwarz, "What's the Connection between Residential Segregation

and Health?," Culture of Health Blog, April 3, 2018, https://www.rwjf.org/en
/blog/2016/03/what_s_the_connectio.html.

17. David Brooks, *The Second Mountain: The Quest for a Moral Life* (Random
House, 2019).

18. David Brooks, "The Threads of Life," *Ideas*, June 5, 2019, https://www.aspen
institute.org/longform/ideas-the-magazine-of-the-aspen-institute-summer-2019
/the-threads-of-life/.

19. Lydia Denworth, *Friendship: The Evolution, Biology, and Extraordinary Power of
Life's Fundamental Bond* (W. W. Norton, 2020).

20. Denworth, *Friendship*, chap. 9.

21. Ben Healy, "How to Make Friends, According to Science," *The Atlantic*
(September 2018): https://www.theatlantic.com/magazine/archive/2018/09/how
-to-make-friends/565742/.

22. Lydia Denworth, *Friendship: The Evolution, Biology, and Extraordinary Power of
Life's Fundamental Bond* (W. W. Norton, 2020).

23. Susan Pinker, *The Village Effect: How Face-to-Face Contact Can Make Us Healthier and Happier* (Random House, 2014).

CHAPTER 6. SINGLE-FAMILY HOUSING

1. Bipartisan Policy Center, *Healthy Aging Begins at Home* (Bipartisan Policy
Center, 2016), https://bipartisanpolicy.org/wp-content/uploads/2019/03/BPC
-Healthy-Aging-Summary.pdf.

2. US Department of Commerce, *2015 Characteristics of New Housing*
(Washington, DC: US Department of Commerce, 2015), https://www.census.gov
/construction/chars/pdf/c25ann2015.pdf.

3. Joint Center for Housing Studies of Harvard University, *Housing America's
Older Adults 2019* (Joint Center for Housing Studies of Harvard University, 2019),
https://www.jchs.harvard.edu/sites/default/files/Harvard_JCHS_Housing
_Americas_Older_Adults_2019.pdf.

4. Richard Florida, "How Housing Wealth Transferred from Families to Corpo-
rations," Bloomberg CityLab, October 4, 2019, https://www.bloomberg.com/news
/articles/2019-10-04/the-decline-in-owner-occupied-single-family-homes.

5. Joint Center for Housing Studies of Harvard University, *Housing America's
Older Adults*.

6. Candace Taylor, "A Growing Problem in Real Estate: Too Many Too Big
Houses," *Wall Street Journal*, March 21, 2019, https://www.wsj.com/articles/a
-growing-problem-in-real-estate-too-many-too-big-houses-11553181782.

7. See the website of Universal Living Laboratory—www.udll.com—for more information.

8. More information on CAPABLE is available at https://nursing.jhu.edu/faculty _research/research/projects/capable/.

CHAPTER 7. **APARTMENTS**

1. Anne DiNardo, "All Ages Welcome," *Environments for Aging Magazine* (Spring 2017): 27–31.

2. "Renters and Owners," National Multifamily Housing Council, accessed January 12, 2021, https://www.nmhc.org/research-insight/quick-facts-figures/quick -facts-resident-demographics/renters-and-owners/.

3. "Household Characteristics," National Multifamily Housing Council, accessed December 4, 2020, https://www.nmhc.org/research-insight/quick-facts-figures /quick-facts-resident-demographics/household-characteristics/.

4. "Apartment Turnover Rate Continues to Fall," CBRE, July 30, 2019, https:// www.cbre.us/research-and-reports/US-Multifamily-Research-Brief---Apartment- Turnover-Rate-Continues-to-Fall-July-2019.

CHAPTER 9. **SENIOR LIVING**

1. "How Much Care Will You Need?," US Department of Health and Human Services, last modified October 15, 2020, https://longtermcare.acl.gov/the-basics /how-much-care-will-you-need.html.

2. "Life in a Senior Living Community," American Seniors Housing Association, updated May 18, 2020, https://www.whereyoulivematters.org/life-senior-living -community/.

3. Michele Lerner, "Life Plan Communities Offer Another Alternative to Aging in Place," *Washington Post*, April 16, 2020, https://www.washingtonpost.com/real estate/life-plan-communities-offer-another-alternative-to-aging-in-place/2020/04 /15/d4b42288-729a-11ea-87da-77a8136c1a6d_story.html.

4. Glen A. Tipton, "No More Ghettos: Time for Intergenerational Living," American Institute of Architects, March 29, 2016, https://www.aia.org/articles/3331 -no-more-ghettos-time-for-intergenerational-li:61?tools=true.

5. American Seniors Housing Association, *State of Seniors Housing 2019* (American Seniors Housing Association, 2019), https://www.seniorshousing.org/product /the-state-of-seniors-housing-2019/.

6. Irina Lupa, "RENTCafé National Rent Report: The Average Apartment Rent Was $1,468 in February," RENTCafé, March 2020, https://www.rentcafe

.com/blog/rental-market/apartment-rent-report/february-2020-national-rent
-report/.

7. "Cost of Care Survey," Genworth, last updated December 2, 2020, https://
www.genworth.com/aging-and-you/finances/cost-of-care.html.

8. "Cost of Care Survey."

9. Hospital and Healthcare Compensation Service, *Assisted Living Salary and Benefits Report* (Hospital and Healthcare Compensation Service, 2016).

10. Tami Kamin Meyer, "Colleges and Retirement Communities Partner to Offer Multigenerational Living," Next Avenue, March 20, 2019, https://www.nextavenue
.org/colleges-retirement-communities-partner-multigenerational-living/.

11. For more on Horizon House, visit their website at https://horizonhouse.org/.

12. Jill Vitale-Aussem, *Disrupting the Status Quo of Senior Living: A Mindshift* (Health Professions Press, 2019).

13. Rhéda Adekpedjou et al., "'Please Listen to Me': A Cross-Sectional Study of Experiences of Seniors and Their Caregivers Making Housing Decisions," *PLoS One* 13, no. 8 (2018): e0202975, doi:10.1371/journal.pone.0202975.

14. See the Find and Compare tool on the Medicare website at https://www
.medicare.gov/care-compare/.

15. "Maryland COVID-19 in Congregate Facility Settings," Maryland.gov, last updated December 9, 2020, https://coronavirus.maryland.gov/pages/hcf-resources.

CHAPTER 10. EMERGING OPTIONS, FROM COHOUSING TO TINY HOMES

1. "Real-Life 'Golden Girls?' Why More Seniors Are Living with Roommates," Today.com, July 3, 2019, https://www.today.com/video/real-life-golden-girls-why
-more-seniors-are-living-with-roommates-63219781797.

2. Jacqueline Tempera, "Roxbury Woman in Her 60s and Boston University Student in Her 20s Forge Friendship through Home Sharing Program," MassLive, July 19, 2019, https://www.masslive.com/boston/2019/07/roxbury-woman-in-her
-60s-and-boston-university-student-in-her-20s-forge-friendship-through-home
-sharing-program.html.

3. Sarah Susanka, *The Not So Big House: A Blueprint for the Way We Really Live* (Taunton Press, 2009).

4. Frederick Kunle, "Va. Launching Portable Housing for Aging Relatives," *Washington Post*, May 6, 2010, https://www.washingtonpost.com/wp-dyn/content
/article/2010/05/05/AR2010050503074.html.

5. Ann Marie Shambaugh, "Carmel Considers Easing Process of Building Accessory Dwellings to Address Housing Option Shortage," Current, August 9, 2020,

https://youarecurrent.com/2020/08/09/carmel-considers-easing-process-of
-building-accessory-dwellings-to-address-housing-option-shortage/.

CHAPTER 11. LIVING WITH OR NEAR FAMILY

1. Michael Schwirtz and Lindsey Rogers Cook, "These N.Y.C. Neighborhoods
Have the Highest Rates of Virus Deaths," *New York Times,* May 18, 2020, https://
www.nytimes.com/2020/05/18/nyregion/coronavirus-deaths-nyc.html.

2. Henry Cloud and John Townsend, *Boundaries: When to Say Yes, How to Say No
to Take Control of Your Life* (Zondervan, 1992).

CHAPTER 12. PLACE AS A HUB FOR TECHNOLOGY

1. *House and Home Exhibit,* National Building Museum, Washington, DC, 2019.

2. Klaus Schwab, "The Fourth Industrial Revolution: What It Means, How to Respond," World Economic Forum, January 14, 2016, https://www.weforum.org /agenda
/2016/01/the-fourth-industrial-revolution-what-it-means-and-how-to -respond/.

3. Laurie M. Orlov, "Voice, Health and Wellbeing 2020: The Sounds of Healthcare Change," Aging in Place Technology Watch, January 2020, https://www.agein
placetech.com/files/aip/Voice%20Health%20and%20Wellbeing%202020%20Final
%20-%201-5-2020.pdf.

4. Janet Rae-Dupree, KHN, "Doctor Alexa Will See You Now: Is Amazon Primed
to Come to Your Rescue?," Fierce Healthcare, July 29, 2019, https://www.fierce
healthcare.com/tech/doctor-alexa-will-see-you-now-amazon-primed-to-come-to
-your-rescue.

5. Randy Rieland, "How Social Robots Could Help Older Patients Help Themselves," *Forbes,* April 1, 2019, https://www.forbes.com/sites/nextavenue/2019/04/01
/how-social-robots-could-help-older-patients-help-themselves/?sh=3da7fb117f6d.

6. Joseph Coughlin, "You Are a Cyber Threat to Your Mother in Retirement,
Here's How," *Forbes,* December 17, 2019, https://www.forbes.com/sites/joseph
coughlin/2019/12/17/you-are-a-cyber-threat-to-your-mother-in-retirement-heres
-how/?sh=34a8aeb411a8.

CHAPTER 13. PLACE AS A HUB FOR HEALTH

1. Barbra Mann Wall, "History of Hospitals," Penn Nursing, accessed December 5,
2020, https://www.nursing.upenn.edu/nhhc/nurses-institutions-caring/history-of
-hospitals/.

2. "Intermountain Healthcare Is Now Providing Hospital-Level Care in Patient
Homes," Intermountain Healthcare, June 4, 2020, https://intermountainhealthcare
.org/news/2020/06/intermountain-healthcare-is-now-providing-hospital-level
-care-in-patient-homes/.

3. "Report on the Environment: Indoor Quality," US Environmental Protection Agency, accessed January 12, 2020, https://www.epa.gov/report-environment /indoor-air-quality.

4. Catherine O. Ryan, William D. Browning, Joseph O. Clancy, Scott L. Andrews, and Namita B. Kallianpurkar, "Biophilic Design Parameters: Emerging Nature-Based Parameters for Health and Well-Being in the Built Environment," *International Journal of Architectural Research* 8, no. 2 (2014): 62–76.

5. "Cost of Care Survey," Genworth, last updated December 2, 2020, https:// www.genworth.com/aging-and-you/finances/cost-of-care.html.

6. "Cost of Care Survey."

7. "How Much Care Will You Need," US Department of Health and Human Services, last modified October 15, 2020, https://longtermcare.acl.gov/the-basics /how-much-care-will-you-need.html.

8. See the website of the MedStar Health House Call Program at www.medstar housecall.org.

CHAPTER 14. MAKING THE MOST OF YOUR CURRENT PLACE

1. Marie Kondo, *The Life-Changing Magic of Tidying Up: The Japanese Art of Decluttering and Organizing* (Ten Speed Process, 2014).

2. "Intermountain Healthcare Is Now Providing Hospital-Level Care in Patient Homes," Intermountain Health, June 4, 2020, https://intermountainhealthcare.org /news/2020/06/intermountain-healthcare-is-now-providing-hospital-level-care-in -patient-homes/.

CHAPTER 15. SELECTING A NEW PLACE

1. Robert F. Wiseman, "Why Older People Move: Theoretical Issues," *Research on Aging* 2, no. 2 (1980): 141–54, doi:10.1177/016402758022003.

2. Sarah Gilbert, Elaine Amella, Barbara Edlund, and Lynne Nemeth, "Making the Move: A Mixed Research Integrative Review," *Healthcare* 3, no. 3 (2015): 757–74, doi:10.3390/healthcare3030757.

CONCLUSION. CHOOSING THE RIGHT PLACE AT THE RIGHT TIME

1. Wendell Berry, *Jayber Crow* (Berkeley, CA: Counterpoint, 2001).

2. Definition from "Ageing: Ageism," World Health Organization, November 2, 2020, https://www.who.int/westernpacific/news/q-a-detail/ageing-ageism.

3. Ashton Applewhite, *This Chair Rocks: A Manifesto against Ageism* (Networked Books, 2016).

INDEX